COMPANION PLANTING IN RAISED BED AND CONTAINER GARDENS

GROW CHEMICAL-FREE VEGETABLES, FRUITS, FLOWERS, AND HERBS - FIND THE BEST SOIL MATES FOR ORGANIC PEST CONTROL AND GROW YOUR OWN FOOD YEAR ROUND

MORGAN JACOBS

Copyright © 2024 by Morgan Jacobs

All rights reserved.

No part of this book may be reproduced in any form or by any electronic or mechanical means, including information storage and retrieval systems, without written permission from the author, except for the use of brief quotations in a book review.

This publication is designed to provide accurate and authoritative information in regard to the subject matter covered. It is sold with the understanding that neither the author nor the publisher is engaged in rendering legal, investment, accounting or other professional services. While the publisher and author have used their best efforts in preparing this book, they make no representations or warranties with respect to the accuracy or completeness of the contents of this book and specifically disclaim any implied warranties of merchantability or fitness for a particular purpose. No warranty may be created or extended by sales representatives or written sales materials.

The advice and strategies contained herein may not be suitable for your situation. You should consult with a professional when appropriate. Neither the publisher nor the author shall be liable for any loss of profit or any other commercial damages, including but not limited to special, incidental, consequential, personal, or other damages.

CONTENTS

Introduction	vii
1. GARDEN ALLIES: LAYING THE FOUNDATION	1
The Basics of Companion Planting	2
The Benefits & Why it Works	4
Decoding the Language of Plants	7
Planning Your Companion Planting Garden	9
Tools & Resources for the Modern Gardener	15
2. ELEVATING GARDENS: THE RISE OF RAISED BEDS	21
Designing Your Raised Bed Garden	22
Choosing Containers for Your Garden	25
Best Soil Mixes for Raised Beds & Containers	28
Maximizing Space in Small Gardens	32
D.I.Y Raised Beds & Containers	35
3. THE SYMPHONY OF THE SOIL: MASTERING PLANT FAMILIES	43
Companion Planting for Pest Control	47
Plants That Should Never Grow Together	51
Companion Plants for Pollinators	54
Companion Planting for Soil Health	57
4. THE HARMONY OF HARVEST: VEGETABLE COMPANIONS FOR BOUNTIFUL GARDENS	63
Fruitful Companions	67
Herb Companions & Their Uses	70
Companion Flowers for Vegetable Gardens	73
The Role of Cover Crops	77
5. GROW YOUR OWN FOOD: BUILD A SELF SUSTAINING GARDEN	81
Companion Planting in Permaculture	83
Attracting Beneficial Insects	86

Vertical Companion Planting   89
Companion Planting with Aquaponics   92

6. ROOT WISDOM: NURTURING YOUR GARDENS   99
Mulching Types & Techniques   102
Natural Fertilizers for a Healthy Garden   106
Pruning & Harvesting   109
Managing Pests Naturally   112

7. SPRING INTO GARDENING: A FRESH START FOR COMPANION PLANTING   117
Summer Maintenance Tips   120
Fall Planting & Preparation   124
Winter Care for Raised Beds & Containers   126
Year-Round Harvest Strategies   130

8. TROUBLESHOOTING: THE MOST COMMON GARDEN ISSUES   135
Addressing Common Plant Diseases   136
Solving Watering Issues   138
Nutrient Deficiencies and How to Fix Them   141
Dealing with Overcrowding   144
Rebalancing Your Garden's Ecosystem   147

9. NURTURING THE FOUNDATION: SOIL & SUSTAINABILITY   151
Creating a Seed Saving Plan   156
Encouraging Natural Predators   159
Water Conservation Tips   163
Long-Term Garden Planning   166

Outro   171
References   173

BONUS

INTRODUCTION

Have you ever marveled at the sheer joy and satisfaction that comes from nurturing a garden? There's something genuinely magical about coaxing life from the soil, especially when you're working with limited space. That's where the wonder of companion planting comes into play, transforming your gardening into an orchestra of cooperation and mutual benefit.

Companion planting is not just a method; it's a dance of nature that allows plants to support each other. It's about growing chemical-free produce, naturally managing pests, and squeezing every bit of potential from your raised beds and container gardens. This age-old practice is the secret sauce to maximizing yields and ensuring your little garden thrives, even in the most compact urban spaces.

My journey into the heart of gardening wasn't overnight. It took one wilted tomato plant, struggling in solitude, to open my eyes to the power of companionship in the garden. That moment sparked a passion in me, a desire not just to grow but to grow smarter. It's this passion I'm eager to share with you, especially if you're just dipping your toes into the gardening world.

This book is your guide to understanding and implementing companion planting in your raised beds and container gardens. From selecting the perfect plant pairs to nurturing a self-sustaining ecosystem right in your backyard or balcony, I've distilled everything I know into simple, actionable steps. You'll learn not just the "how" but the "why" behind each pairing, equipping you with the knowledge to make informed decisions about your garden.

This book Is crafted with the urban gardener in mind, offering solutions that are as accessible as they are effective. Through clear guidance, I aim to demystify gardening and make it a joy, not a chore.

I understand the hurdles that can intimidate new gardeners. Fear of failure, confusion over where to start, or doubts about your green thumb (or lack thereof) might loom large. But here's the thing: gardening is a journey of discovery, filled with both triumphs and learning curves. Through this book, I'll be right there with you, turning challenges into victories and aspirations into realities.

Structured to ease you into gardening, the book unfolds in a series of chapters that build on each other, from setting up your garden and choosing your plants to maintenance and harvesting. Expect practical tips, real-world examples, and perhaps a few laughs along the way. We'll explore everything with the help of illustrations, charts, and even QR codes that bring additional resources right to your fingertips.

Now, let me share a quick story. Last spring, I paired basil with my tomatoes in a container, not expecting much. To my surprise, not only did the basil thrive, but the tomato plants were the healthiest I'd ever grown. This small success was a revelation and a testament to the power of companion planting.

So, consider this book not just a resource but an invitation to join a community of fellow garden enthusiasts. Together, we'll navigate the ups and downs of gardening, supporting each other along the way.

This isn't just about growing plants; it's about growing together, savoring the beauty and bounty that your garden will bring to your life.

Ready to begin? Let's turn these pages into fertile soil from which your gardening dreams can grow. Welcome to the journey.

1

GARDEN ALLIES: LAYING THE FOUNDATION

IN THE HEART of a bustling city amidst the concrete jungle, there's a balcony where tomatoes and basil thrive together, sharing space and resources. This isn't by chance but by choice—a choice rooted in the ancient practice of companion planting. This method, which might seem like a quaint throwback, is actually a powerful tool for modern gardeners, especially those working with limited space in urban environments.

THE BASICS OF COMPANION PLANTING

Long before the advent of commercial fertilizers and pesticides, farmers across the globe observed that certain plants, when grown together, helped each other thrive. This observation laid the groundwork for what we now recognize as companion planting. Its origins can be traced back to various indigenous practices, such as the Native American "Three Sisters" technique, where corn, beans, and squash are grown together, each plant offering support, nutrients, or protection to the others.

Companion planting, at its core, is about creating plant communities where mutual support leads to a flourishing garden. This symbiotic relationship is not a new concept. Historical records suggest that the Greeks and Romans practiced companion planting, and it was commonplace in cottage gardens across medieval Europe. These gardens were not just for show; they were vital for sustaining families, with every plant serving a purpose, either nutritional or medicinal.

Core Principles

The practice of companion planting is guided by a few foundational principles, such as spatial interactions—how plants use physical space to benefit each other. For instance, tall plants provide shade for shorter, shade-tolerant plants during the hottest parts of the day. Temporal considerations also play a role; different plants have varying growth cycles and can be planned in a way that they don't compete for resources at the same time.

Understanding these principles requires a shift in perspective. Traditional gardening often focuses on the individual plant. At the same time, companion planting considers the garden as a whole, an ecosystem where plants interact with each other and their environment in complex ways.

Scientific Backing

Skeptics might wonder if companion planting is more folklore than science, but numerous studies back its effectiveness. Research has shown that certain plant combinations can deter pests, improve soil health, and increase yield. For example, a study published in the "Journal of Ecology and The Natural Environment" found that intercropping specific crop pairs reduced pest populations without the need for chemical pesticides. This is just one of many studies that validate the benefits of companion planting, offering a scientific basis for age-old practices.

Gardener's Mindset

Embracing companion planting requires gardeners to adopt a holistic view, observing and experimenting to discover what works best in their unique garden conditions. It's about noticing how plants affect each other and adjusting plans based on those observations. This iterative process is not unlike cooking, where a chef adjusts recipes based on taste and available ingredients. Similarly, gardeners tweak their plant combinations based on the results they observe, creating a tailored garden ecosystem that thrives.

In essence, companion planting invites gardeners to become keen observers and creative experimenters. It's a method that celebrates diversity, encourages sustainability, and builds a deep connection with the natural world. Through understanding its basics, history, and scientific foundations, gardeners are equipped to transform their gardens—no matter the size—into vibrant, healthy ecosystems.

THE BENEFITS & WHY IT WORKS

The allure of companion planting isn't just in its history or the satisfaction it brings but in the tangible benefits it offers to gardeners, especially those working within the constraints of smaller urban spaces. These benefits span from enhanced plant growth and natural pest control. It will improve soil health and promote biodiversity. Each element contributes to a garden that's not just surviving but thriving.

Enhanced Growth

The notion that plants can positively affect the growth of their neighbors is fascinating. It's about more than just physical support, like tall sunflowers providing shade for lettuce during the midday heat. It's about the unseen, underground exchanges and aerial interactions that fuel growth. For instance, legumes have the remarkable ability to fix atmospheric nitrogen, a crucial nutrient, making it available in the soil for neighboring plants. This partnership between legumes and non-legumes can lead to more robust growth in the latter, a benefit that synthetic fertilizers struggle to replicate without the risk of over-fertilization and the subsequent harm to local waterways.

Another aspect of enhanced growth comes from the strategic placement of plants to maximize their access to sunlight, a critical factor in photosynthesis. When taller plants are positioned to give just enough afternoon shade to those that are prone to wilting under intense sun, both plants can photosynthesize at optimal levels, leading to healthier, more productive gardens.

Natural Pest Control

One of the most compelling reasons gardeners gravitate towards companion planting is its capacity for managing pests naturally. This benefit is twofold: certain plants can directly repel pests through their scent or chemical compounds, while others attract beneficial insects that will help fight common garden pests.

Marigolds, with their bright blooms, are a classic example, emitting a fragrance that deters nematodes and other pests from nearby vegetables. Similarly, the humble basil plant, when grown alongside tomatoes, can help repel flies and mosquitoes, reducing the reliance on chemical pesticides. This not only keeps the garden healthier but also protects the beneficial insects that contribute to a balanced ecosystem.

The role of "trap crops" in natural pest control cannot be overstated. These sacrificial plants attract pests away from more valuable crops, effectively saving them from damage. Nasturtiums, for instance, can draw aphids away from peppers and tomatoes, acting as a decoy that allows the main crop to flourish unscathed.

Improved Soil Health

Soil is the foundation of any garden, and its health is paramount for the success of the plants it nurtures. Companion planting plays a vital role in maintaining and improving soil health through several mechanisms. The diversity of root systems in a well-planned companion garden helps prevent soil compaction, allowing for better water infiltration and air circulation within the soil. This diversity also supports a broader range of soil microorganisms, which are essential for decomposing organic matter and making nutrients available to plants.

Cover crops, often used in companion planting schemes, play a critical role in soil health. By covering bare soil, they help prevent erosion from wind and rain. Once cut down and left to decompose, cover crops will add organic matter back into the soil. It will act as a green manure that enriches the soil for future plantings.

Moreover, the practice of rotating companion plants from season to season can help break cycles of pests and diseases that thrive in monocultures, further contributing to soil health. This rotational practice ensures that specific soil-borne pathogens don't build up over time, protecting future crops.

Increased Biodiversity

A garden teeming with a variety of plant life is not just a visual delight; it's a bustling ecosystem that supports a wide range of life forms. Companion planting inherently promotes biodiversity, both in the plant species grown and the beneficial insects and animals attracted to the garden. This diversity creates a more resilient garden ecosystem capable of withstanding fluctuations in the environment, pest pressures, and disease outbreaks.

Diverse plantings offer varied habitats and food sources, encouraging beneficial predators such as ladybugs, lacewings, and birds to take residence in the garden. These natural predators keep pest populations in check, reducing the need for intervention.

The increased biodiversity also contributes to pollinator health. By providing a succession of blooms throughout the growing season, companion planting ensures that pollinators have a consistent source of nectar and pollen. This not only supports the local pollinator population but also enhances the garden's productivity through improved pollination.

In essence, the benefits of companion planting mirror the principles of nature itself—diversity leads to resilience, cooperation leads to abundance, and attention to the natural world's cues leads to sustainability. Through companion planting, gardeners can create microcosms of nature's balance, yielding not just crops but a deeper connection with the ecosystem at large.

DECODING THE LANGUAGE OF PLANTS

Plants possess an intricate communication network, invisible to the naked eye yet pivotal for their survival and growth. This dialogue, hidden beneath the soil or carried in the air, is essential for the thriving of companion plants in any garden setting. Let's explore the depths of these interactions, from chemical signals and physical support to the unseen synergy of root systems and the dance of pollination that ensures the continuation of plant species.

Chemical Communications

Plants emit a variety of chemical signals, both above and below ground, serving as distress calls, repellents, or attractants. These chemical messages can enhance their growth or protect them from pests. A well-documented phenomenon is the release of volatile organic compounds (VOCs) when a plant is under attack. These VOCs can signal neighboring plants to strengthen their defenses preemptively, a remarkable testament to plant interconnectivity. For example, when pests attack tomato plants, they release a chemical that can prompt nearby plants to produce substances that are less palatable or toxic to the invaders. This chemical warfare doesn't just stop at defense strategies; it also involves attracting beneficial insects that act as natural predators to the pests. Marigolds, with their distinctive scent, are champions at this, secreting compounds into the soil that ward off nematodes and above-ground pests, making them invaluable allies in a companion-planted garden.

Physical Interactions

Beyond the realm of chemical exchanges, plants also support each other through physical means. The concept of a living trellis, where taller plants like sunflowers or corn provide a natural support structure for climbers like beans or cucumbers, is a prime example. This not only maximizes vertical space but also reduces the risk of diseases by improving air circulation around the plants. Furthermore, the canopy formed by larger plants offers shade to those beneath, protecting them from the harsh midday sun and conserving moisture in the soil. This shading technique is particularly beneficial for leafy greens, which tend to bolt or wilt in intense heat, extending their growing season and productivity.

Root Systems Synergy

Beneath the soil's surface, a complex network of roots intertwines, creating an underground web of support and exchange. The interactions between root systems of companion plants can lead to enhanced nutrient uptake, improved water retention, and even protection against soil-borne pathogens. Legumes, for instance, harbor nitrogen-fixing bacteria in their root nodules, converting atmospheric nitrogen into a type that plants can use. This natural fertilization process benefits neighboring plants, enriching the soil with a critical nutrient for plant growth. Meanwhile, deep-rooted plants like carrots can break up compacted soil, making it easier for neighboring plants with shallower roots to access water and nutrients. This root system synergy exemplifies the unseen cooperation that lies at the heart of effective companion planting.

Pollination Partnerships

The act of pollination is a delicate dance between plants and their pollinator partners, crucial for the production of fruits and seeds. The placement of companion plants can significantly impact pollination success, with specific arrangements attracting more pollinators or facilitating the transfer of pollen. Flowers play a vital role in this process, drawing in bees, butterflies, and other pollinators with their vibrant colors and enticing scents. By interspersing flowering plants like lavender or borage among crops, gardeners can create a buzzing hub of activity, ensuring that their vegetable flowers receive ample attention from pollinators. Additionally, planting in blocks rather than single rows can make it easier for pollinators to find and move among the flowers, increasing the chances of pollination. This strategic placement not only benefits the crops but also supports the health of local pollinator populations, creating a win-win situation for the garden and the environment.

In the intricate world of companion planting, understanding the language of plants opens up new avenues for creating harmonious and productive gardens. From the chemical signals that orchestrate communal defenses to the physical and underground partnerships that bolster growth and health, every interaction is a testament to the interconnectedness of nature. As gardeners, tapping into this natural network allows us to cultivate spaces that are not only bountiful but also resilient and sustainable, echoing the complex ecosystems found in the wild.

PLANNING YOUR COMPANION PLANTING GARDEN

When you decide to create a companion planting garden, the first step is identifying your ambitions. Maybe you're aiming to pull as much produce as possible from a tiny plot, or perhaps you're more interested in having a garden that's a haven for beneficial insects.

Your goals might also include growing herbs that will make your culinary experiments more exciting. Setting straightforward objectives will not only guide your gardening efforts but also help measure your success as the seasons change.

Setting Goals

Reflect on what you want from your garden. Is it about self-sufficiency? Or is it the joy of seeing a variety of colors and textures flourishing together? Maybe it's both. Knowing what you're after makes the next steps smoother and more focused. If pest control is a priority, you'll lean towards plants known for their repellant properties. On the other hand, if you're after a continuous supply of fresh veggies, planning for succession planting becomes crucial.

Choosing Your Plants

Selecting the right plants is like picking characters for a play where everyone needs to get along and bring out the best in each other. Start with what you like to eat or see in your garden, then narrow down your choices based on their compatibility. Some plants are good neighbors, sharing nutrients and fending off each other's pests, while others can stunt each other's growth or attract the same diseases. Consider the adult size of the plants to ensure they won't overshadow each other, blocking sunlight or hogging nutrients.

- *Compatibility:* Research which plants are beneficial companions. For example, tomatoes do well with basil and marigolds but should steer clear of potatoes and fennel.
- *Space Considerations:* Factor in the mature size of each plant to prevent overcrowding and competition for sunlight.
- *Personal Preferences:* Grow what you love. There's no point

in dedicating space to eggplants if no one in the family eats them.

Garden Layout

Designing your garden layout is akin to sketching a blueprint that balances sunlight, airflow, and aesthetics. A successful layout ensures that each plant receives the right amount of sun and shade, has sufficient space to grow, and is placed strategically to benefit its neighbors. Start with a simple sketch, noting areas that receive full sun versus partial shade.

- *Sunlight:* Position taller plants on the north side so they don't cast shadows on shorter plants.
- *Accessibility:* Ensure that every plant is easily reachable for maintenance and harvesting.
- *Aesthetics:* Arrange plants in a way that's pleasing to the eye, mixing colors, textures, and heights for visual interest.

Raised beds and containers offer flexibility in arranging your garden layout. They can be positioned to maximize sun exposure and moved if necessary. Plus, they provide excellent drainage, which is crucial for healthy plant growth.

Succession Planting

Succession planting is the strategic timing of plantings to extend the harvest season. By planning your garden in waves, you can enjoy fresh vegetables from spring through fall. Start with cool-season crops like lettuce and peas, followed by warm-season favorites such as tomatoes and peppers. As one crop finishes, another takes its place, keeping your garden productive.

- *Early Season:* Begin with cool-weather crops that can be planted before the last frost.
- *Mid-Season:* Transition to warm-weather vegetables and herbs after the danger of frost has passed.
- *Late Season:* Plant fall-harvest crops in late summer, ensuring a bounty well into the cooler months.

This method not only maximizes your garden's yield but also helps manage pests and diseases by disrupting their life cycles.

Cool Season Crops Not Affected By Frost

Cabbage & Kale	Collard Greens	Garlic	Horseradish	Brussel Sprouts
Asparagus	Kohlrabi	Leek	Broccoli	Onions & Shallots
Rhubarb	Pea & Broad Bean	Radish	Spinach	Turnip

Cool Season Crops Affected by Frost

Beets	Carrots	Cauliflower	Celery	Lettuce
Chard	Chinese Cabbage	Swiss Chard	Endive	Potato
Mustard	Parsnip			

Warm Season Crops

New Zealand Spinach	Cantaloupe	Pepper	Sweet Potato	Pumpkin
Squash	Sweet Corn	Cucumber	Snap Bean	Tomato
Watermelon	Eggplant	Lima Bean		

To pinpoint the ideal planting times, first, figure out which "zone" you reside in. The United States is divided into 13 distinct planting zones, each with its own recommended planting schedules.

You can find your specific zone by inputting your zip code on several free websites. To find my gardening zone, I used a website called "Garden in Minutes." To access the site, simply scan this QR code.

Raised Beds and Containers

Choosing the proper containers and designing your raised beds is vital for the success of your garden. They should be both functional and aesthetically pleasing, fitting into the space you have available and complementing the surrounding environment.

- *Raised Beds:* Ideal for vegetables and herbs, raised beds improve drainage, reduce strain on your back, and can be topped up with a soil mix tailored to your plant's needs. Consider materials like untreated wood or stone to match your garden's style. Heights can vary, but a depth of 12-18 inches accommodates most plants.

- *Containers:* Perfect for patios or balconies, containers come in various sizes and materials. Choose pots with enough depth for the roots of your chosen plants and ensure they have drainage holes to prevent waterlogging. Lightweight materials like fabric pots or resin are easier to move and can be a good choice for gardeners who like to rearrange their plants.

When planning your raised beds and containers, think about the following:

- *Location:* Place them where they will receive the optimal amount of sunlight based on the needs of the plants you intend to grow.

- *Soil:* Use a high-quality potting mix that can give you the perfect balance of drainage and water retention. Consider adding compost to enrich the soil.
- *Watering Needs:* Evaluate the water requirements of your plants and plan your garden layout accordingly. Grouping plants with others that share similar watering needs can make maintenance easier.

Incorporating these elements into your garden planning sets the stage for a thriving companion planting system. It ensures that your plants have the best possible start, are positioned to support each other, and ultimately, contribute to a vibrant, productive garden.

TOOLS & RESOURCES FOR THE MODERN GARDENER

In the realm of companion planting, having a suitable set of tools and resources can make all the difference. From the tangible—spades and shears—to the intangible—knowledge and community support—each plays a crucial role in cultivating a garden that's both productive and joyful. Here's a closer look at what you'll need to bring your companion planting garden to life and keep it thriving.

Essential Gardening Tools

A gardener's toolkit is a personal assortment shaped by the specifics of their garden and their approach to tending it. However, certain tools are universally invaluable:

- *Spade and Trowel:* These are indispensable for digging and planting. A spade is perfect for breaking ground and turning soil, while a trowel is ideal for more precise tasks like planting seedlings and bulbs.

- *Pruning Shears:* Essential for keeping plants healthy and well-shaped, these are used to trim and shape plants, remove dead or diseased foliage, and harvest herbs and vegetables.
- *Garden Fork:* This tool is excellent for loosening, lifting, and turning over soil, which is crucial for preparing your beds for planting.
- *Watering jugs or Hoses with a Spray Attachment:* Regular, gentle watering is vital to a healthy garden. Choose a can or hose attachment that allows for a soft, shower-like spray to avoid damaging young plants.
- *Gloves:* Protect your body from thorns, splinters, and dirt. A good pair of gloves can also provide a better grip on tools.
- *Wheelbarrow:* For more extensive gardens, a wheelbarrow is invaluable for moving soil, compost, and plants with ease.

With these tools in hand, you're well-equipped to start laying the groundwork for your companion planting garden. Keeping them clean and well-maintained will ensure they last for many seasons to come.

Online Communities

The internet is a treasure trove of information and support for gardeners. Engaging with online communities can offer insights, advice, and encouragement from fellow gardening enthusiasts. Here are some platforms where you can connect with others:

- *Gardening Forums:* Websites like GardenWeb and the Gardening section of Reddit are bustling with discussions on every gardening topic imaginable, including companion planting. You can ask people questions and get advice from others who have faced similar gardening challenges.

- *Social Media Groups:* Facebook and Instagram are home to many gardening groups and pages where members post photos of their gardens, share tips, and offer support. Look for groups focused on organic gardening, urban gardening, or specifically on companion planting.
- *YouTube Channels:* Many gardeners and horticulturists share their knowledge through video tutorials on YouTube. Channels like Epic Gardening and MIgardener offer practical advice that's visually engaging and easy to follow.

By utilizing these resources, you are gaining access to a wealth of knowledge and becoming part of a global community of gardeners who share your passion.

Apps and Technology

The digital age has brought a suite of tools that can simplify the complexities of gardening, from planning your garden layout to identifying pests. Consider incorporating these apps into your gardening practice:

- *Garden Planner Apps:* Apps like From Seed to Spoon and the Old Farmer's Almanac Garden Planner help you design your garden layout, choose plants that will grow well together, and schedule planting and harvesting times.
- *Plant Identification Apps:* Unsure about a plant in your garden or a pest that's causing damage? Apps like PictureThis and PlantNet allow you to snap a photo and get instant information on plant species and common pests.
- *Gardening Guides and Trackers:* Apps such as GrowIt! and GardenTags offer plant care guides, gardening tips, and the ability to track your garden's progress. They also have social features for sharing with and learning from other gardeners.

Whether you're a beginner gardener or have years of experience under your belt, these resources can provide you with new perspectives and deepen your understanding of companion planting. They serve as a reminder that gardening is both an art and a science, one that rewards patience, curiosity, and a willingness to learn.

As you start on your companion planting journey, remember that the most valuable resource at your disposal is your own observation and intuition. Paying attention to how your plants interact with each other and responding to their needs will guide you toward a bountiful and beautiful garden.

2

ELEVATING GARDENS: THE RISE OF RAISED BEDS

IMAGINE TRANSFORMING a patch of concrete into a lush, productive garden. This might sound like a modern-day miracle, but it's entirely possible with raised bed gardening. This method isn't just about overcoming space constraints; it's a celebration of creativity, optimization, and the sheer joy of growing more with less. Raised beds can turn balconies, patios, and even the tiniest of urban spaces into thriving gardens. The secret? It's all in the setup. From choosing suitable materials to understanding the dance of sunlight and shadow, every decision propels your garden closer to success.

DESIGNING YOUR RAISED BED GARDEN

Raised bed gardens are like mini-ecosystems, custom-built to fit your gardening dreams. They offer a world of benefits, transforming challenges into opportunities, whether it's poor soil quality or limited space that you're dealing with. Let's walk through the essentials of setting up your raised bed garden, ensuring it becomes a cornerstone of growth and joy.

Benefits of Raised Beds

Raised beds come with a suite of advantages that can make gardening more accessible and enjoyable:

- *Improved Drainage:* Say goodbye to soggy roots. Raised beds allow water to drain efficiently, keeping your plants happy even in heavy rain.
- *Enhanced Soil Quality:* Fill your beds with the perfect soil mix tailored to your plant's needs. This can be a game-changer in areas with less-than-ideal native soil.
- *Easier Pest Management:* Elevated soil levels and the option to add barriers make it more challenging for critters to snack on your greens.
- *Reduced Strain on Your Back:* No need to bend over too far. Raised beds bring the garden to you, making planting and harvesting more comfortable.

Construction Materials

Choosing the ideal materials for your raised beds is about balancing durability with environmental impact and aesthetics:

- *Wood:* A classic choice, cedar, and redwood offer natural resistance to rot and pests. Avoid treated woods that could leach harmful chemicals into your soil.
- *Stone or Brick:* For a more permanent structure, stone or brick can add stability and a touch of elegance to your garden. Just remember, these materials can be more expensive and labor-intensive to set up.
- *Metal:* Galvanized steel is durable and offers a sleek, modern look. Ensure it's properly sealed to prevent rust.
- *Recycled Materials:* From old bathtubs to repurposed pallets, get creative and give materials a second life as part of your garden.

Optimal Dimensions

Both the size and depth of your raised beds can make a big difference in what you can grow:

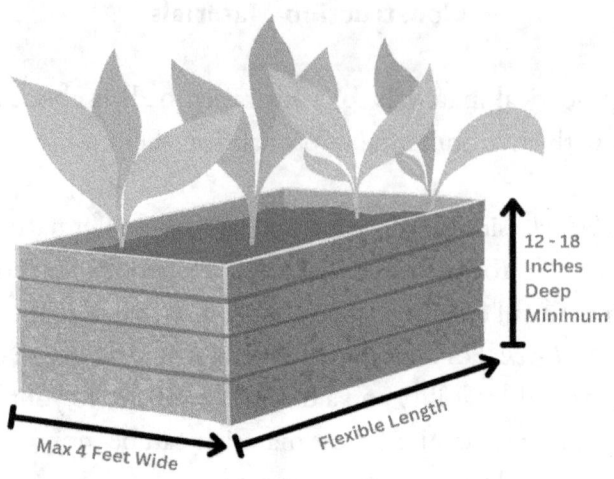

- *Width:* Aim for a maximum of 4 feet wide. This allows you to easily reach the center from either side without overreaching into the bed.
- *Length:* This is flexible, but keep walkability in mind. Long beds may need access points or paths.
- *Depth:* A minimum of 12 inches is recommended, though 18 inches is ideal for deeper-rooted plants.

Location and Orientation

Picking the perfect spot is crucial for maximizing growth:

- *Sunlight:* Most vegetables and herbs crave a minimum of 6 to 8 hours of sun. Observe your space throughout the day to find the sunniest spots.
- *Air Circulation:* Good airflow helps prevent fungal diseases. Avoid tight corners or overly sheltered areas where air might stagnate.
- *Accessibility:* Ensure your beds are easily accessible for

watering, weeding, and harvesting. You're more likely to tend to your garden if it's conveniently located.

By thoughtfully designing your raised bed garden, you lay the foundation for a flourishing green space. It's about making informed choices—from the materials you use to build your beds to their placement and dimensions. This careful planning not only optimizes the health and productivity of your plants but also improves the overall gardening experience, making it more enjoyable and less of a chore. With your raised beds set up, you're well on your way to creating a vibrant, thriving garden that's tailored to your unique space and gardening goals.

CHOOSING CONTAINERS FOR YOUR GARDEN

Picking the suitable container for your garden is akin to selecting a home that best suits your lifestyle and needs. Just as you'd choose a house, the variety, material, and functionality of garden containers play a pivotal role in the well-being of your plants. In this section, we explore the myriad of container options, dissect the benefits and drawbacks of different materials, and highlight the importance of drainage and watering. We will also guide you in choosing companion plants that will coexist harmoniously in the shared space of a container.

Container Varieties

In the world of container gardening, the options are as vast and varied as the plants themselves. From pots and planters to boxes and hanging baskets, each type offers unique advantages for different gardening scenarios.

- *Pots and Planters:* The most common choice, available in a range of sizes to suit everything from herbs to small trees.
- *Window Boxes:* Ideal for those with limited space, they can add a hit of color to windowsills or balconies.
- *Hanging Baskets:* Perfect for trailing plants, adding vertical interest to your garden space.
- *Grow Bags:* Lightweight and versatile, grow bags are great for root vegetables and can be easily moved or stored.

Each type of container can serve a specific purpose in your garden, whether it's to maximize space, grow a particular kind of plant, or simply add aesthetic value.

Material Considerations

The material of your container can significantly affect the health of your plants and the overall maintenance of your garden.

- *Plastic*: Lightweight and cost-effective, plastic pots are versatile but can degrade over time in sunlight. They retain moisture well, which is beneficial for thirsty plants but may require extra drainage for others.
- *Terracotta*: These classic clay pots are porous, allowing air and water to pass through, which helps prevent root rot. However, they can dry out quickly and are vulnerable to cracking in cold temperatures.
- *Fabric*: A newer option, fabric pots promote air pruning of roots and excellent drainage. They are also lightweight and can be folded away when not in use.
- *Metal*: Durable and stylish, metal containers can get very hot in direct sunlight, potentially stressing plants. Ensure they're used in suitable locations or for plants that thrive in warm conditions.

Each material brings its own set of pros and cons, impacting everything from water retention to temperature control. Your choice needs to align with the specific needs of the plant and the environmental state of your garden space.

Drainage and Watering

Proper drainage is the cornerstone of successful container gardening. Without it, water can pool at the bottom of your container, leading to root rot and other water-related diseases. Here are a few tips to ensure your container garden remains well-drained and adequately watered:

- Ensure all containers have holes at the bottom. If your chosen container doesn't come with pre-drilled holes, make some yourself using a drill or a nail and hammer.
- Add a layer of gravel or pottery pieces at the base of your pots before adding soil. This can help prevent the drainage holes from getting clogged with soil.
- Consider self-watering containers for busy gardeners. These containers have a built-in reservoir that allows plants to take up water as needed, reducing the frequency of watering.

Balancing moisture levels in container gardens requires regular attention, as containers can dry out faster than traditional gardens, especially during hot weather. Regular checks will help you maintain the optimal moisture level for your plants.

Plant Compatibility

When it comes to companion planting in containers, not all plants play nice. Selecting plants that thrive together in the confined space of a container is crucial for their mutual success.

- *Consider Growth Habits*: Pair tall plants with those that spread out or trail down the sides to maximize space and reduce competition.
- *Complementary Needs*: Choose plants with similar water and sunlight requirements to ensure one doesn't outcompete the other.
- *Beneficial Relationships*: Some plants can deter pests from their companions or even enhance their flavor when grown together.

Research and planning are critical to successful companion planting in containers. By carefully selecting compatible plants, you can create a mini ecosystem in each container, where every plant supports and benefits from its neighbors. This approach not only maximizes the health and yield of your plants but also turns each container into a microcosm of cooperative living, reflecting the broader principles of nature's interconnectedness.

As you delve into the world of container gardening, remember that each choice—from the type and material of the container to the plants that call it home—shapes the microenvironment of your garden. With thoughtful selection and care, containers offer a flexible, creative, and highly rewarding avenue for bringing your gardening aspirations to life, no matter the size of your space.

BEST SOIL MIXES FOR RAISED BEDS & CONTAINERS

Navigating the world of soil for raised beds and containers might seem like decoding a complex puzzle. Yet, getting this right means setting the stage for your garden's success. Each plant in your companion planting scheme benefits from a nurturing environment that begins with the soil. It's the medium that supports their roots, offers nutrition, and maintains moisture. Understanding soil composition, crafting your own mixes, employing organic amendments, and maintaining soil health over time are pivotal steps in this process.

Soil Composition

A harmonious blend of nutrients, pH, and texture forms the backbone of any prosperous garden soil. Here's a breakdown:

- *Nutrients:* Plants need a mix of macronutrients (nitrogen, phosphorus, potassium) and micronutrients (calcium, magnesium, iron) for growth and health.
- *PH Level:* Most garden plants thrive in soil with a pH between 6.0 and 7.0, though some prefer more acidic or alkaline conditions. Testing your soil's pH is vital to ensure it meets your garden's needs.
- *Texture:* Good garden soil has a balance of sand, silt, and clay, contributing to what gardeners call "loam" – soil that holds moisture but drains well. For containers and raised beds, ensuring adequate drainage while retaining moisture is vital.

DIY Soil Mixes

Creating your soil mix allows you to tailor the growing medium to your garden's specific requirements. Here are a couple of recipes to get started:

Basic Raised Bed Mix:

- One part compost provides organic matter and nutrients.
- One part topsoil acts as the primary medium.
- One part coarse sand or perlite enhances drainage.

Container Mix for Leafy Greens:

- Two parts peat moss or coconut coir retains moisture.
- One part compost supplies nutrients.
- One part vermiculite aids in moisture retention and aeration.
- A handful of bone meal provides phosphorus for root development.

Adjust these mixes based on your plants' needs. For instance, plants that prefer well-drained soil might benefit from extra perlite or sand, while acid-loving plants will appreciate a mix with more peat moss.

Organic Amendments

Incorporating organic matter into your soil mix not only improves its structure but also boosts its fertility. Here are some amendments to consider:

- *Compost:* The all-star of organic amendments, compost enriches the soil with a broad spectrum of nutrients and beneficial microorganisms.
- *Worm Castings:* A gentle, nutrient-rich amendment that also improves soil structure.
- *Bone Meal:* A great source of phosphorus, essential for root development.
- *Green Sand:* Supplies potassium and micronutrients and improves moisture retention.

Amendments should be mixed thoroughly into your soil. A rule of thumb is to refresh your soil mix with these organic enrichers at the start of each planting season or as needed.

Maintenance and Refreshing Soil

Over time, soil in raised beds and containers can become compacted and depleted of nutrients, impacting plant health. Here's how to keep your soil vibrant:

- *Aeration:* Periodically loosening the soil helps prevent compaction and allows roots to breathe. In containers, be gentle to avoid damaging the roots.
- *Top-Dressing:* Each season, add a fresh layer of compost or your chosen amendments to replenish nutrients. This is especially important in containers, where nutrient depletion happens more rapidly.
- *Crop Rotation:* Rotating plant families in your raised beds can help manage nutrient depletion and pest pressures. For example, follow nitrogen-fixing legumes with nutrient-hungry brassicas.
- *Cover Crops:* Planting cover crops in raised beds during the off-season can protect and enrich the soil. Legumes like clover add nitrogen, while deep-rooted plants like daikon radish can break up compacted layers.

Maintaining the health of your soil is an ongoing process, integral to the success of your garden. By giving careful attention to the blend and upkeep of your soil, you create a nurturing foundation that supports the diverse needs of your companion plants. This commitment to soil health not only maximizes the productivity and vitality of your garden but also aligns with sustainable gardening practices, ensuring your little slice of nature thrives for seasons to come.

MAXIMIZING SPACE IN SMALL GARDENS

When space is at a premium, every inch of your garden becomes precious. Yet, limitations often spark the most creative solutions. For those of us tending to our green aspirations in the cozy confines of urban dwellings, the quest to grow more in less space is both a challenge and an adventure. This section delves into ingenious ways to expand your garden's potential, making every square foot count.

Vertical Gardening

Elevating your garden quite literally takes your plants to new heights. Vertical gardening techniques not only save on precious ground space but also add an unexpected dimension of beauty to small areas. Here's how you can implement this approach:

- *Trellises and Climbing Frames:* Perfect for vining plants like peas, beans, and some types of squash. These structures can be leaned against walls or balconies, offering a backdrop of greenery.
- *Wall Planters and Living Walls:* Transform bare walls into lush vertical gardens. Modular planters that can be stacked or arranged to fit your space and aesthetic preferences are available.
- *Hanging Baskets:* Ideal for trailing varieties of tomatoes, strawberries, or vibrant flowers. They can be suspended from balconies, window ledges, or even overhead structures.
- *Shelving Units:* A simple set of shelves can host a variety of pots, creating a tiered garden effect. Ensure each shelf gets enough light, or use grow lights to supplement.

Incorporating these vertical elements not only maximizes your growing area but also turns your garden into a captivating visual feature of your home.

Interplanting Strategies

Interplanting, or growing multiple types of plants together in the same space, is akin to assembling a diverse team where each member brings unique strengths to the table. This method enhances the use of space and fosters a supportive environment among different species. Here's how to apply it effectively:

- *Complementary Growth Patterns:* Pair tall plants that crave sunlight with shorter, shade-tolerant ones. This ensures both can thrive without competing for light.
- *Harvest Timing:* Combine fast-growing crops with those that take longer to mature. By the time the slower plants need more room, the quicker ones will have been harvested.
- *Root Depth Variation:* Plant deep-rooted vegetables alongside those with shallower roots. This allows them to draw nutrients from different soil levels without interference.

Thoughtfully selected companions can lead to a denser, more productive garden, with plants that protect and enrich each other.

Container Mobility

The ability to move containers offers a strategic advantage in small-space gardening. This mobility allows you to adapt to your plant's needs and the changing seasons. Here's why movable containers can be a game-changer:

- *Optimal Sun Exposure:* Shift your plants to catch the sun as its position changes, ensuring they get the light they need to flourish.
- *Protection from Elements:* Easily move plants to sheltered spots during harsh weather, be it scorching sun, heavy rain, or cold snaps.
- *Pest Management:* If pests target a particular plant, isolate it by moving the container away, preventing the spread to other plants.

Using casters, trolleys, or lightweight containers makes this process effortless, keeping your garden flexible and responsive to its inhabitants' needs.

Creative Space Solutions

Exploring novel ways to utilize every nook and cranny of your available space can turn even the smallest of areas into a verdant oasis. Here are some inventive ideas:

- *Rail Planters:* Perfect for balconies, these planters sit snugly over railings, providing a space-saving solution for herbs and flowers.
- *Pallet Gardens:* An upcycled pallet can serve as an excellent vertical garden for lettuce, herbs, and small flowers. Lean it against a wall or hang it up to save floor space.
- *Gutter Gardens:* Repurposed gutters attached to walls or under windowsills offer a creative trough for growing herbs and succulents.
- *Furniture Planters:* Old furniture pieces, like dressers or bookshelves, can be transformed into unique planters, with each drawer or shelf hosting different plants.

By viewing your space through a lens of possibility, every potential spot becomes an opportunity to grow something. This approach not only maximizes your garden's productivity but also infuses your living space with life and greenery, turning the challenge of limited space into an exploration of creativity. Through vertical gardening, interplanting, movable containers, and inventive use of space, the smallest gardens can yield surprising abundance and beauty, proving that even in the most compact urban settings, nature finds a way to thrive.

D.I.Y RAISED BEDS & CONTAINERS

Creating your own raised beds and containers is a rewarding venture that can be tailored to fit not only your garden's environmental needs but also its aesthetic. This endeavor doesn't require you to be a master carpenter or to have a hefty budget. With some essential tools, a bit of creativity, and a willingness to get your hands dirty, you can build functional and unique homes for your plants.

Step-by-Step Building Guides

Building a Simple Raised Bed:

1. *Materials Needed:* Four 2x6 boards (length depends on desired bed size), wood screws, drill, saw, measuring tape, and a level.
2. *Cutting the Boards:* If not pre-cut, saw your boards to the desired length for the four sides of your bed. Two pairs of equal lengths work best.
3. *Forming the Frame:* Lay out the boards in your desired shape, aligning the ends to form corners—pre-drill holes to

prevent wood splitting and screw the boards together at each corner.
4. *Positioning:* Place the frame in your chosen spot. Use the level to ensure the ground is even. If not, remove or add soil underneath until level.
5. *Filling:* Add a mix of topsoil, compost, and any other amendments your plants may need. Water the soil thoroughly before planting.

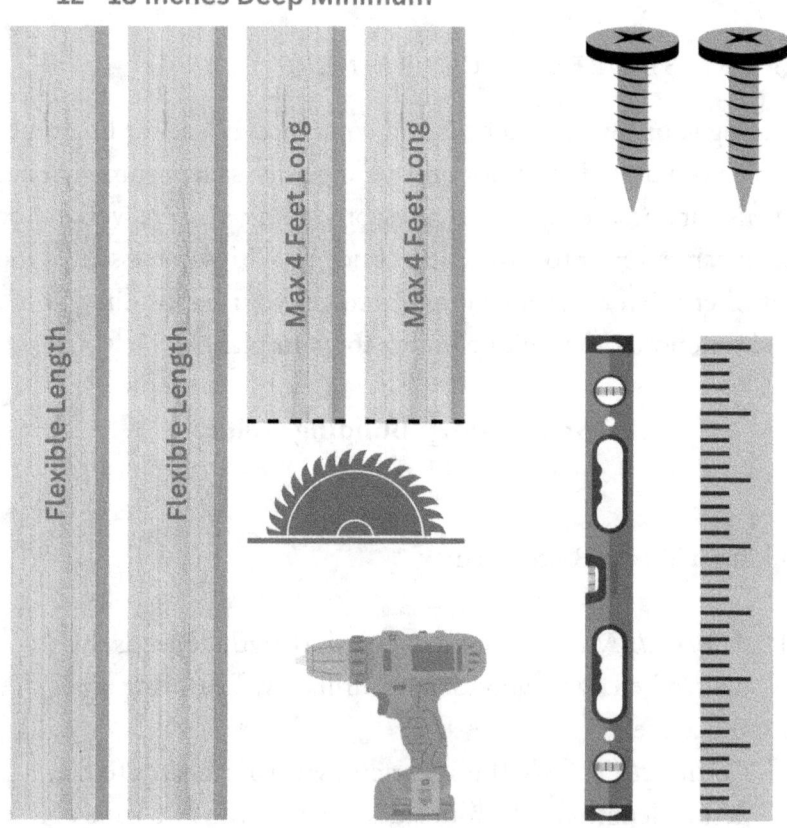

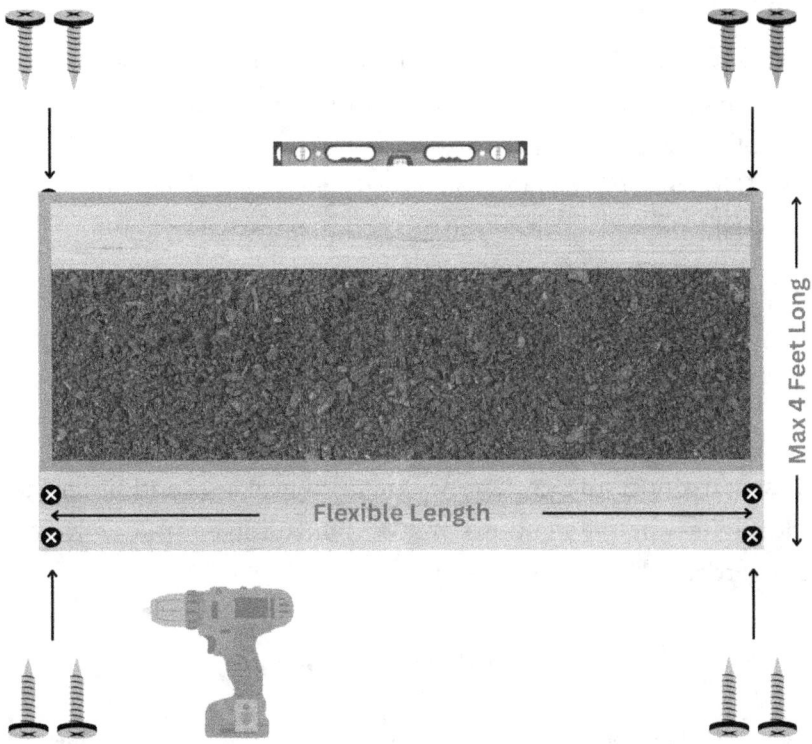

Crafting a Container from Repurposed Items:

1. *Choosing a Container:* Almost anything can be turned into a plant container—old buckets, barrels, even furniture. Ensure it's deep enough for your plant's roots.
2. *Creating Drainage Holes:* Use a drill to make several holes in the bottom of the container. If the material is rigid, like metal, you may need a specific drill bit.
3. *Preparing for Planting:* Add a layer of gravel or broken pottery shards at the bottom to facilitate drainage. Fill with a suitable potting mix, leaving space at the top for planting.

Upcycling Ideas

- *Old Tires:* Stack them up and fill them with soil for a durable, raised planting area. Painting them can add a splash of color to your garden.
- *Wooden Pallets:* Stand them vertically for a space-saving planting wall or dismantle them to use the wood for constructing beds.
- *Kitchen Colanders:* These make whimsical hanging baskets with built-in drainage. Just add a strong hook for hanging and a coconut coir liner.

These ideas not only save money but also give a second life to items that might otherwise end up in a landfill, adding a unique touch to your garden.

Cost-Saving Tips

- *Seek Out Free Materials:* Many businesses give away pallets or crates that can be repurposed into garden beds or containers.
- *Buy Soil in Bulk:* If filling large raised beds, purchasing soil and compost in bulk rather than in bags can offer significant savings.
- *Share Resources:* Team up with friends or neighbors to purchase materials in bulk and share the costs, as well as the bounty from your gardens.

A little resourcefulness goes a long way in stretching your garden budget without cutting corners on quality.

Customization for Companion Planting

When you build your own raised beds and containers, you have the freedom to design them specifically for the plants you intend to grow together. Here's how to ensure your construction supports companion planting:

- *Adjustable Dividers:* In larger raised beds, use removable wooden dividers to create compartments for different plant pairings. This flexibility allows you to rotate or change pairings with ease.
- *Multi-Level Containers:* For containers, consider building or choosing tiered options that allow plants with similar water and light needs to be grouped together, optimizing their growing conditions.
- *Strategic Placement:* Construct your raised beds and containers so they can be easily moved or rotated to meet the changing sun exposure and growth patterns of your companion plants.

Customizing your garden structures in this way ensures that the specific needs of your companion plant pairings are met, fostering a harmonious and productive garden ecosystem.

Taking the DIY route for your raised beds and containers not only saves money but also offers the satisfaction of crafting a garden space that's uniquely yours. It's an opportunity to blend creativity with functionality, resulting in a garden that reflects your personal style and meets the needs of your plants.

Whether it's through the thoughtful design of raised beds that encourage healthy plant relationships or the inventive repurposing of materials for containers, the essence of DIY gardening is about embracing possibilities and making the most of what you have. As we move forward, remember that the true beauty of gardening lies not just in the harvest but in the journey of growth, learning, and connection with the natural world around us.

3

THE SYMPHONY OF THE SOIL: MASTERING PLANT FAMILIES

PICTURE A BUSTLING ORCHESTRA, each musician tuning their instrument, readying themselves for a harmonious performance. Now, imagine your garden as such an orchestra, with each plant family representing a section of musicians, from the strings to the brass, all poised to play a symphony that breathes life into your garden. This chapter turns the spotlight on understanding the dynamics between different plant families, focusing on how they can harmoniously coexist, share nutrients, and support each other's growth while avoiding competition. It's about fine-tuning your garden's performance to achieve a balance that resonates with vitality and abundance.

Group Dynamics

In the intricate dance of companion planting, recognizing the unique attributes and needs of different plant families sets the stage for successful harmonization. Just like in an orchestra where the strings section complements the woodwinds, certain plant families naturally enhance each other's growth when paired together. This synergy is often rooted in their nutrient requirements, growth patterns, or pest resistance, making some combinations particularly beneficial.

Leafy Greens and Root Vegetables are great role models. The leafy members of the Brassicaceae family, like kale and cabbage, enjoy the company of root vegetables such as carrots and beets from the Apiaceae family. While the leafy greens utilize the upper layer of the soil, the root vegetables delve deeper, minimizing competition for nutrients.

Nutrient Sharing

Imagine two neighbors sharing a meal; one provides the main course, and the other brings dessert. In a similar vein, certain plant families share nutrients through their root systems in a way that ensures both get a well-rounded meal. This nutrient exchange can significantly boost their growth and yield.

Legumes can be paired with almost anything. Legumes (members of the Fabaceae family) are the generous hosts of the garden party, fixing atmospheric nitrogen into the soil, which is a crucial nutrient for all plants. Pairing legumes with heavy feeders like corn or squash results in a mutual benefit, as the legumes provide the nitrogen these plants crave.

Companion Examples

Real-life examples of successful pairings can serve as inspiration for your garden's composition. Here are a few classic duos that highlight the concept of mutual benefit:

- *Tomatoes and Basil:* Beyond being a culinary match made in heaven, tomatoes (Solanaceae family) and basil (Lamiaceae family) are great garden companions. Basil helps repel pests that might fancy tomato plants, and some gardeners swear it even improves the tomatoes' flavor.
- *Legumes with Brassicas:* As mentioned, legumes enrich the soil with nitrogen, which is eagerly absorbed by members of the Brassicaceae family. This pairing not only maximizes soil fertility but also optimizes space usage.

This is just the tip of the iceberg. Scan this QR code to access a full companion planting PDF guide!

Avoiding Competition

While some plants play well together, others can be likened to musicians playing out of sync, disrupting the garden's harmony. Recognizing which plant families to keep apart is as crucial as knowing which to pair. Plants that vie for the same nutrients, light, or space can hinder each other's growth, leading to a less productive garden.

- *Onions and Beans:* Onions (and their relatives in the Allium family) can be a hindrance to the growth of beans (Fabaceae

family) due to the release of certain compounds that beans find disagreeable.
- *Tomatoes and Corn:* Both are heavy feeders, and tomatoes and corn compete fiercely for soil nutrients, particularly nitrogen, leading to subpar growth for both if planted too closely.

In the grand orchestra that is your garden, understanding the dynamics of plant families and their companions is akin to conducting a symphony. It's about orchestrating a performance where each plant plays to its strengths, supported by its neighbors, resulting in a garden that's not only productive but also a testament to the beauty of mutual support and balance in nature. By tuning into the needs and benefits of different plant families, gardeners can create a harmonious space where every plant thrives, contributing to a bountiful and healthy harvest.

COMPANION PLANTING FOR PEST CONTROL

In the realm of gardening, pests are akin to uninvited guests at a party, turning up where they're least wanted. But rather than reaching for chemical pesticides, imagine having a guest list that naturally keeps the party crashers at bay. That's the essence of using companion planting for pest control. This approach involves selecting plants that either repel unwanted insects or attract beneficial ones, creating a garden that's both productive and harmonious.

Natural Repellents

Some plants are the garden's knights, armed with natural defenses that repel specific pests. These botanical protectors release scents or substances that pests find disagreeable, effectively keeping them at a distance.

- *Marigolds:* The cheerful blooms of marigolds do more than brighten your garden; they release a scent that deters nematodes and even rabbits. Planting marigolds around your vegetable garden acts like a natural shield, protecting your crops from these common nuisances.
- *Garlic:* Known for its strong aroma, garlic is a powerhouse when it comes to repelling pests, including aphids and Japanese beetles. Interspersing garlic among roses or raspberries can help keep these plants free from pests without the need for chemical interventions.

Incorporating these natural repellents into your garden not only keeps pests at bay but also adds diversity and color, enhancing the garden's aesthetic appeal.

Trap Cropping

Think of trap cropping as setting up a decoy at your garden party. It involves planting a crop that's particularly attractive to pests, drawing them away from your main crops. Once the pests congregate on the trap crop, you can remove them from your garden, either by hand or by treating the trap crop with organic pest control methods.

- *Nasturtiums:* Acting as a magnet for aphids, nasturtiums can be planted around fruit trees or vegetable gardens to lure aphids away from your prized plants.
- *Sunflowers:* These towering beauties can attract stink bugs away from tomatoes and peppers. Planting sunflowers on the perimeter of your garden can keep stink bugs occupied, reducing their numbers on your main crops.

This strategic placement of plants can significantly reduce pest populations, safeguarding the health of your garden without harming the environment.

Beneficial Insects

In every garden's story, there are heroes and villains. Beneficial insects are the heroes, preying on the pests that threaten your plants. Certain companion plants can act as beacons, attracting these beneficial predators to your garden, where they help maintain a natural balance.

- *Sweet Alyssum:* This fragrant flower is a favorite among ladybugs, which are voracious eaters of aphids and mites. Planting sweet alyssum around lettuce or beans can help keep aphid populations in check.
- *Dill:* Besides being a culinary delight, dill attracts beneficial wasps that prey on cabbage worms and other caterpillars. Planting dill near tomatoes or cabbage can enhance protection against these common pests.

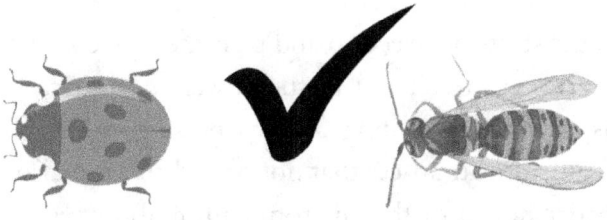

By inviting these beneficial predators into your garden, you're enlisting nature's own pest control service, reducing the need for manual intervention and building a healthier garden ecosystem.

Examples

Real-world examples serve as proof of the effectiveness of companion planting for pest control. Here are a couple of success stories that illustrate the concept in action.

- *A Community Garden in Oregon:* Faced with a persistent aphid problem, this community garden implemented a companion planting strategy, introducing nasturtiums and sweet alyssum around their vegetable plots. Within a season, they observed a significant reduction in aphid populations, with an increase in ladybugs and other beneficial insects.
- *A Vineyard in California:* To combat grapevine pests, a vineyard incorporated marigolds and garlic around the perimeter of their grapevines. The result was a noticeable decrease in nematode activity and fewer instances of pests like leafhoppers, contributing to a healthier vineyard and a more robust grape yield.

These examples highlight the practical benefits of companion planting for pest control, demonstrating how gardeners and farmers alike can leverage natural relationships between plants and insects to create more resilient and productive growing environments.

In essence, the strategic selection and placement of companion plants for pest control is a testament to the power and intricacy of natural ecosystems. By understanding and harnessing these relationships, gardeners can cultivate spaces that not only thrive but also contribute to the broader health of the environment, embodying principles of sustainability and harmony. Through natural repellents, trap cropping, and the attraction of beneficial insects, we can protect our gardens from pests in a way that's safe, effective, and in tune with nature's rhythms.

PLANTS THAT SHOULD NEVER GROW TOGETHER

Gardening, much like hosting a dinner party, involves knowing which guests will spark joyous conversations and which might not get along. In the garden, this knowledge helps prevent unintentional plant feuds that can hinder growth, spread disease, or even lead to plant casualties. Understanding the dynamics of allelopathy, resource competition, disease propagation, and specific incompatible combinations is crucial for maintaining a peaceful and thriving garden.

Allelopathy

Imagine a plant with a secret weapon, a chemical it releases into the soil that says, "This is my space." That's allelopathy, a biological phenomenon where certain plants release substances that can inhibit the growth, survival, and reproduction of other plants. These biochemicals, known as allelochemicals, serve as a natural defense mechanism, ensuring the plant's dominance in its territory. For gardeners, planting allelopathic plants without awareness of their effects can lead to unexpected challenges.

- *Black Walnut:* The king of allelopathic plants, black walnut trees produce juglone, a compound harmful to many garden plants like tomatoes, potatoes, and blueberries. Planting these sensitive species within the root zone of a black walnut tree can spell disaster.
- *Sunflowers:* While beautiful and beneficial in many ways, sunflowers also exhibit allelopathic properties, releasing substances that can suppress the growth of nearby plants, making them poor neighbors for potatoes and pole beans.

Resource Competition

In every garden, there's a silent battle for resources: light, water, and nutrients. When plants with similar appetites are placed too closely, they vie for these essentials, often to the detriment of one or both species. This competition can lead to stunted growth, reduced yield, and, in some cases, the demise of the weaker plant.

- *Corn and Tomatoes:* Both are heavy feeders, craving a lot of nitrogen. Planted together, they compete for this vital nutrient, leading to poor development and yield.
- *Cucumbers and Aromatic Herbs:* Cucumbers need a lot of water, while many aromatic herbs, like sage and thyme, prefer drier conditions. Grouping them together can result

in overwatering the herbs or underwatering the cucumbers, compromising their health.

Disease Propagation

Certain plant families are susceptible to the same diseases, and when planted too close to each other, they can create a hotspot for disease outbreaks. This proximity allows diseases to spread more rapidly, potentially wiping out your efforts in those categories.

- *Nightshades (Tomatoes, Peppers, Eggplants, and Potatoes)*: These relatives share vulnerabilities to blights and wilts. Planting them in close succession can lead to the swift transfer of diseases, impacting the entire group.
- *Squash and Melons:* Both are prone to powdery mildew. If one gets infected, the disease can quickly jump to the other if they're neighbors, leading to a garden-wide issue.

Incompatible Combinations

In the plant world, not all pairings are made in heaven. Some plants, when placed together, can lead to mutual suffering due to their conflicting needs or adverse reactions to each other.

- *Onions and Beans:* Onions, part of the allium family, can stunt the growth of beans and peas. The alliums emit substances that legumes find particularly hostile, leading to a poor harvest.
- *Brassicas (Cabbage, Cauliflower, Kale) and Strawberries:* Brassicas can inhibit the growth of strawberries. The soil enriched for brassicas does not suit strawberries, which thrive in slightly acidic conditions, leading to an unhappy coexistence.

In the vibrant tapestry that is a garden, each plant plays a role, contributing to the overall beauty and bounty. However, like any community, understanding the relationships and dynamics between its members is vital to ensuring harmony and prosperity. By recognizing which plants should keep their distance, gardeners can avoid the pitfalls of allelopathy, resource competition, disease propagation, and incompatible combinations, fostering a garden where every plant has the opportunity to thrive.

COMPANION PLANTS FOR POLLINATORS

In the heart of every blooming garden, a silent yet vibrant exchange occurs, where flowers and pollinators engage in a dance as old as time itself. This section shines a light on the crucial role companion plants play in attracting and sustaining the diverse pollinator populations that breathe life into our gardens. Our focus here is not just on creating a space that bursts with color and fragrance but one that serves as a sanctuary for bees, butterflies, and other pollinators, ensuring the continuity of bloom and fruit year after year.

Attracting Pollinators

Choosing the right companion plants to attract pollinators is akin to setting up a welcome sign in your garden. These plants are the unsung heroes, offering nectar and pollen as irresistible treats for visiting bees, butterflies, and other beneficial insects. To turn your garden into a pollinator paradise, consider these tips:

- Favor a range of plants that are known for their attractiveness to pollinators. Lavender, with its fragrant purple spikes, is a magnet for bees, while the vibrant blooms of zinnias draw in butterflies and hummingbirds.

- Incorporate native plants into your garden. These local varieties are often more appealing to native pollinators and are well-adapted to the local climate and soil conditions.
- Don't overlook the importance of herbs. Many flowering herbs, such as oregano, thyme, and borage, offer rich sources of nectar when they bloom. As a bonus, they provide fresh flavors for your kitchen.

Successive Blooming

To keep pollinators coming back, your garden needs to offer a continuous buffet of blooms from early spring through late fall. This concept, known as successive blooming, ensures that at any given point in the growing season, something is flowering in your garden. Here's how to achieve this:

- Plant a mix of early bloomers, summer stars, and late flowers. Crocuses and snowdrops kick off the season, followed by mid-season bloomers like coneflowers and sunflowers, and ending with asters and goldenrods as the cool weather sets in.
- Pay attention to the bloom time information on plant tags or seed packets to help stagger plantings for a season-long display.
- Remember, some plants, once their primary bloom is done, can be deadheaded to encourage a second bloom, extending their attractiveness to pollinators.

Habitat Creation

Beyond just food, pollinators need safe places to nest and overwinter. Creating habitats that cater to these needs can encourage them to take up shelter in your garden, ensuring their presence throughout the seasons. Here's what you can do to make your garden a haven for pollinators:

- Leave some areas of your garden wild. Patches of bare ground, piles of twigs, and undisturbed plant debris can offer nesting sites for ground-nesting bees and other insects.
- Consider installing bee hotels or butterfly houses to provide shelter. These can be simple DIY projects that not only serve a purpose but also add a decorative touch to your garden.
- Ensure a water source is available. A shallow dish with stones or marbles for bees and butterflies to land on will help prevent drowning while they drink.

Pollinator-Friendly Pairings

Some companion plant pairings go above and beyond in creating an environment that's particularly welcoming to pollinators. By pairing these plants, you amplify their benefits, creating a lush, productive, and vibrant ecosystem right in your backyard. Here are a few pairings to consider:

- *Sunflowers and Lavender:* Sunflowers tower above, providing the perfect landing spots for bees, while lavender at their base fills the air with its calming scent, drawing in a crowd of pollinators.
- *Borage and Strawberries:* Borage is a powerhouse for attracting bees, and its presence can boost strawberry yields by improving pollination rates. Plus, borage's vivid blue flowers add a splash of color to the strawberry patch.
- *Catmint and Roses:* Catmint, with its cloud of blue flowers, is a bee favorite and, when planted near roses, can help deter

pests while attracting pollinators, ensuring your roses are well-pollinated and healthy.

In crafting a garden that sings with the buzz of bees, the flutter of butterfly wings, and the vibrant colors of a well-pollinated landscape, we tap into the essence of what it means to garden in harmony with nature. This approach not only brings us bountiful harvests and a riot of color but also plays a part in supporting the health of our local ecosystems, making each garden a cornerstone in the conservation of our planet's precious pollinators. Through thoughtful plant selections, creating nurturing habitats, and fostering environments rich in diversity, we can ensure that our gardens are places of refuge, sustenance, and beauty for the pollinators who play such a vital role in the cycle of life.

COMPANION PLANTING FOR SOIL HEALTH

In the tapestry of a garden, soil is the unseen hero, cradling roots and nurturing life with its complex blend of nutrients and organisms. Just as a musician tunes their guitar to create perfect harmony, gardeners can fine-tune their soil's health through strategic companion planting. This section delves into the ways companion planting can invigorate soil, turning it into a fertile foundation for a thriving garden.

Nitrogen Fixers

Imagine your garden soil as a bustling marketplace where plants exchange nutrients much like traders. In this marketplace, nitrogen-fixing plants are akin to generous benefactors, enriching the soil with nitrogen, an essential nutrient that many plants need in abundance but cannot produce on their own. These plants, primarily from the legume family, have a unique partnership with rhizobia bacteria, enabling them to convert atmospheric nitrogen into forms that plant roots can absorb.

Integrating nitrogen fixers like peas, beans, and clover into your garden not only boosts soil fertility but also supports the growth of neighboring plants. For a harmonious pairing, try planting legumes alongside leafy greens or corn. The greens will benefit from the nitrogen boost, and the corn offers a natural trellis for climbing beans, creating a mutually beneficial relationship.

Root Structures

Diversity in root structures plays a pivotal role in maintaining a healthy soil environment. Just as a choir blends different voices to achieve a full sound, combining plants with varying root depths creates a dynamic soil structure. This variety prevents compaction, allowing roots to navigate freely and soil to retain moisture more effectively.

Consider mixing deep-rooted plants like tomatoes with shallower-rooted herbs and lettuce. The deeper roots break up the soil, making it possible for water and nutrients to reach the roots of all plants involved. This not only enhances soil aeration but also deters soil erosion, keeping your garden's foundation solid and resilient.

Organic Matter

Decaying plant matter is the soil's version of compost, gradually breaking down to enrich the soil with organic nutrients. Companion planting can maximize this natural process. When plants like beans or peas are cut back, leaving their roots in the ground, they decompose and provide valuable organic matter for the soil.

Including a mix of annuals and perennials ensures a continuous supply of organic matter as different plants reach the end of their life cycles at various times. This ongoing cycle of growth and decay feeds the soil, creating a self-sustaining system that minimizes the need for external fertilizers.

Soil Microbes

A vibrant community of soil microbes is crucial for a fertile garden, aiding in decomposition, nutrient cycling, and even protecting plants from pathogens. Diverse plant life encourages a rich microbial ecosystem, which in turn supports healthier, more vigorous plants.

Incorporating a variety of companion plants creates a buffet for these microbes, offering a range of root exudates and organic matter for them to feed on. This diversity not only nourishes the microbial life but also enhances the symbiotic relationships within the soil, promoting a robust and balanced garden ecosystem.

In the garden, every plant, every handful of soil, and every drop of water is part of an intricate ballet of life, with each element playing a crucial role in the health and productivity of the whole. Through companion planting, gardeners can nurture their soil, creating a foundation that is rich in nutrients, well-structured, and teeming with life. This approach not only supports vigorous plant growth but also aligns with the natural cycles of the earth, fostering a garden that is both productive and sustainable.

As we finish this exploration of soil health through companion planting, we're reminded of the interconnectedness of all living things and the vital role soil plays in the garden's ecosystem. By fostering a diverse and vibrant soil environment, we lay the groundwork for a garden that thrives year after year, resilient in the face of challenges and abundant in its offerings.

Moving forward, the principles discussed here pave the way for a deeper understanding of how to sustain and enhance the health of our gardens, not just for our enjoyment but for the benefit of the planet. With a well-tuned soil ecosystem as our foundation, we're ready to explore the next steps in our gardening adventure, confident in the knowledge that a healthy garden starts from the ground up.

4

THE HARMONY OF HARVEST: VEGETABLE COMPANIONS FOR BOUNTIFUL GARDENS

PICTURE THIS: A BUSTLING FARMERS' market on a sunny Saturday morning. Each stall is brimming with vibrant produce, from juicy tomatoes to crisp lettuce, each vegetable telling a story of its journey from seed to harvest. Now, imagine your garden as a miniature version of this market, where every plant thrives, not just in solitude but in the company of friends. This chapter is about turning that vision into reality through the magic of companion planting with vegetables. It's about creating pairings that not only coexist but help each other flourish.

Synergistic Effects

In the vegetable garden, some pairings are like a seasoned dance duo, with each step and turn perfectly synchronized for a stunning performance. These are the combinations that, when grown together, offer mutual benefits, leading to enhanced growth, flavor, and even yield. It's like how beans fix nitrogen in the soil, providing ample nutrition for corn, which in return offers the beans a natural trellis to climb. Or how spinach, when nestled under taller plants, enjoys the cool shade, growing tender leaves even as the summer heats up. These synergistic effects aren't just about survival; they're about helping each plant be its best self.

Spacing and Timing

Even the best of friends need their space, and vegetables are no different. Knowing how close to plant your veggie companions and when to plant them is crucial for their shared success. For instance, radishes can be sown among carrots. The radishes germinate quickly, breaking the soil crust for the slower-germinating carrots. But timing is critical—the radishes will be harvested before the carrots need more room to grow. Here's a quick guide on spacing and timing to ensure your vegetable companions benefit from each other's presence without cramping each other's style:

- *Keep fast-growers and slow-growers in mind:* Plant quick-to-

harvest veggies like lettuce or radishes around those that take longer, like broccoli or brussels sprouts.
- *Use vertical space to your advantage:* Train vining plants like cucumbers up a trellis to free up ground space for low-growers such as strawberries or bush beans.

Remember, some plants, like tomatoes, need more room to flourish, so give them the space they need while interplanting with companions like basil or marigolds that don't mind being a bit closer together.

Water and Light Considerations

Managing the needs for water and light among your vegetable companions ensures everyone gets what they need without overshadowing or out-thirsting each other. It's like planning a group road trip where everyone agrees on the temperature for the car's AC—compromise is key. Squash, with its large leaves, might cast too much shade on sun-loving peppers, so it's better to pair them with something that appreciates a little afternoon shade, like spinach. Here are some tips to keep everyone happy:

- Group together veggies that love a good soak, like celery and lettuce, and keep them separate from those that prefer drier feet, such as oregano and sage.
- Use taller plants to provide intentional shade for those who struggle in the full blast of the sun, but position them so that they don't block out the light completely.

Successful Vegetable Pairings

Finally, for the pièce de résistance, here are some tried and tested vegetable pairings that have been proven to work well together under various conditions. Each pairing is a match made in garden heaven, offering benefits that range from improved pest control to better use of space and nutrients:

- *Tomatoes and Basil:* Not only do these two make a classic culinary pairing, but basil also helps repel pests like mosquitoes and tomato hornworms.
- *Carrots and Spring Onions:* The strong scent of spring onions can deter carrot flies from laying eggs near your precious carrots.
- *Lettuce and Chives:* Chives can help ward off aphids, which are often a nuisance for lettuce growers.
- *Beans and Corn:* Corn offers beans a natural trellis to climb, while beans fix nitrogen in the soil, nourishing the corn.
- *Squash, Corn, and Beans:* Known as the "Three Sisters," this trio supports each other—squash keeps the soil moist, beans provide nitrogen, and corn serves as a support for the beans.

For every gardener, whether you have a sprawling backyard or a few pots on a balcony, these vegetable companions offer a blueprint for a garden that's not just alive but thriving. It's a testament to the power of working together, where each plant contributes to the well-being of its neighbors, creating a lush, productive, and harmonious garden ecosystem.

This is just the tip of the iceberg. Scan this QR code to access a color companion planting PDF guide

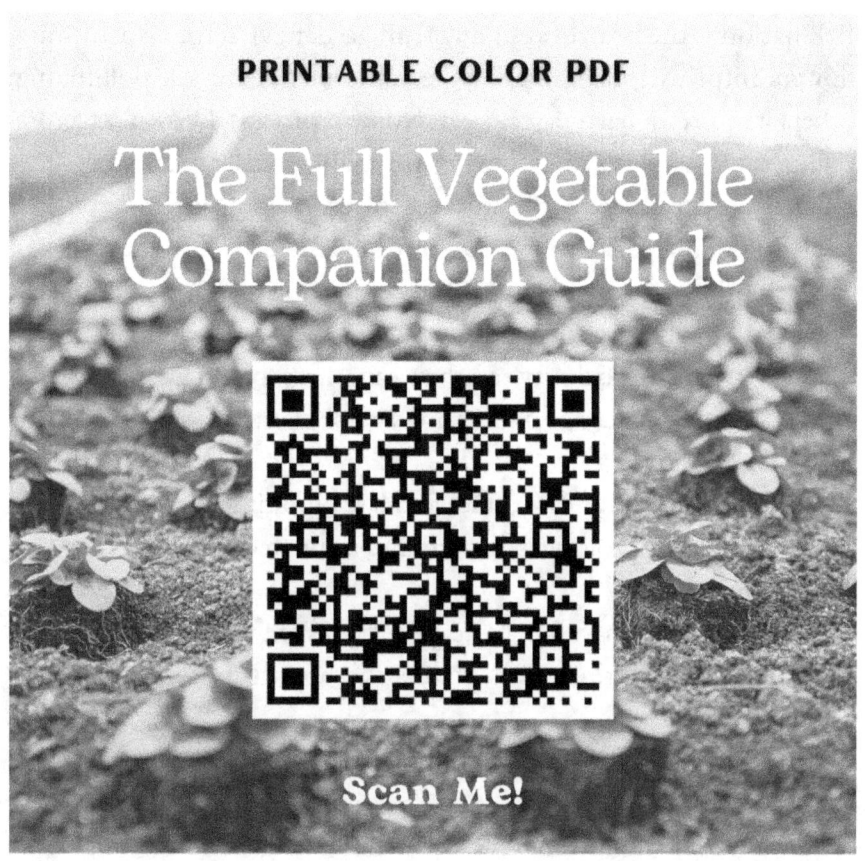

FRUITFUL COMPANIONS

In the realm of gardening, fruit trees and shrubs weave a tale of interdependence and cooperation that can significantly uplift your garden's productivity and health. Much like a well-orchestrated ensemble, where each instrument's unique timbre contributes to the richness of the performance, fruit companions bring out the best in each other through various means. This section explores how to cleverly pair fruit plants to foster a garden that's as fruitful as it is enchanting.

Pollination Partners

Pollination is the heartbeat of any fruit garden, vital for transforming flowers into luscious fruits. While some plants are self-pollinating, others require a partner to bear fruit, a process known as cross-pollination. This is where having the right partner plants becomes crucial. For instance, apple varieties often need a different type of apple to pollinate. Planting a 'Granny Smith' near a 'Honeycrisp' can ensure both trees flourish and produce a bountiful harvest. Similarly, blueberries, which thrive on acidic soil, can benefit from being planted in close proximity, as they can share pollinators like bees, enhancing the chances of pollination across plants.

- *Blueberries* – Pair early, mid, and late blooming varieties together for prolonged harvest and improved cross-pollination.
- *Apples* – Ensure different apple varieties are within bee flight distance to increase cross-pollination opportunities.

Pest Management

Pests can be a significant challenge in fruit gardening, but some ingenious pairings can help manage these unwelcome guests naturally. Certain fruits, when planted alongside specific companions, can either repel pests or attract beneficial insects that act as natural predators of common pests. Strawberries, for example, greatly benefit from the presence of borage, which deters strawberry pests while attracting pollinators. Another practice involves underplanting grapevines with clover, which draws beneficial insects that prey on grape pests.

- *Peaches and Garlic* – Garlic planted at the base of peach trees can help repel peach borers, a common threat to these fruit trees.

- *Raspberries and Marigolds* – Marigolds emit a scent that deters raspberry pests, making them an excellent companion to plant along the perimeter of raspberry patches.

Microclimate Creation

Creating microclimates through strategic pairing can significantly impact the microenvironment around your fruit plants, providing conditions that favor their growth and fruit production. For instance, taller fruit trees can offer shade to lower-growing, shade-tolerant berry bushes, protecting them from the harsh afternoon sun. This not only helps in temperature regulation but also in moisture conservation, creating a more hospitable environment for both plants.

- *Apple Trees and Currant Bushes* – The shade from apple trees can create a cooler understory for currant bushes, which prefer a bit of respite from intense sunlight.
- *Pears and Rhubarb* – Rhubarb benefits from the dappled shade pear trees provide, and in return, its large leaves can help maintain soil moisture around the pear tree's base.

Examples of Fruit Companions

Some fruit pairings stand out for their ability to support each other's growth, improve pollination rates, and even boost each other's defense against pests. These examples serve as a guide for creating fruitful companionships in your garden:

- *Citrus and Avocado* – Planting citrus trees near avocados can aid in creating a humid microclimate, which is beneficial for avocados, which thrive in slightly humid

conditions. The dense foliage of citrus trees can also act as a windbreak, protecting the more sensitive avocado trees.
- *Fig and Pomegranate* – Both thriving in similar climatic conditions, figs and pomegranates can be planted together to create a diverse fruit garden. Their differing root depths allow them to coexist without competing for water and nutrients, making them ideal companions.
- *Kiwi and Grapes* – Kiwi vines require a sturdy support system, which grapevines can provide when grown on robust trellises. This pairing not only optimizes space but also encourages a beneficial sharing of pollinators.

By embracing the principles of companion planting in fruit gardening, you can orchestrate a garden that not only yields an abundance of fruit but also supports a healthier, more sustainable ecosystem. Through thoughtful pairings that consider pollination partners, pest management, microclimate creation, and specific companion examples, your garden can become a testament to the power of collaboration and mutual support in the natural world. Each pairing, carefully selected and nurtured, contributes to a harmonious and productive garden where every plant, from the towering fruit trees to the humble groundcover, plays a vital role in cultivating abundance.

HERB COMPANIONS & THEIR USES

In any garden, herbs act much like the strings in an orchestra, subtly enhancing the performance of their fellow plants with a whisper of aroma and a dash of color. Their roles extend far beyond the kitchen, playing a pivotal part in the health and productivity of the garden through their aromatic properties, soil improvement abilities, and the culinary delights they inspire when paired with a suitable vegetable or fruit. This section peels back the layers of how integrating herbs into your garden can be a game-changer, offering natural protection, enriching the soil, and elevating your dishes from the garden to the table.

Aromatic Protection

The air around your garden is alive with the scents of herbs, each carrying its own secret weapon against pests and diseases. The volatility of their oils makes them formidable protectors of their leafy companions. Mint, with its vigorous growth and potent scent, can deter a wide array of pests, including ants and aphids, while also attracting beneficial insects like hoverflies. Planting mint near cabbages can help keep away the cabbage moth, but remember, mint likes to spread, so keeping it in containers is wise to prevent it from taking over. Similarly, thyme, when nestled among strawberry plants, can fend off worms that favor these sweet berries. Its low-growing habit makes it an ideal living mulch, keeping the soil moist and the strawberries happy.

- Mint near cabbages repels cabbage moths.
- Thyme with strawberries guards against worms.

Soil Improvement

Beyond their protective aromas, some herbs actively contribute to the health of the soil, enriching it with essential nutrients or even improving its structure. Chervil, a delicate herb favored in French cuisine, is known for its deep roots, which help to break up heavy soils, allowing air and moisture to reach the root zones of neighboring plants more effectively. Additionally, its presence has been noted to boost the growth and flavor of radishes planted nearby. Similarly, fennel, while a somewhat particular companion due to its strong allelopathic tendencies, can, when placed correctly, improve the vigor and health of plants around it by attracting beneficial nematodes that prey on soil pests.

- Chervil enhances soil structure and benefits radishes.
- Fennel, used judiciously, attracts beneficial nematodes.

Culinary Pairings

The true joy of gardening comes when it's time to harvest, and what could be more satisfying than gathering a basket of herbs alongside vegetables and fruits that complement each other both in the garden and on your plate? Basil and tomatoes are a classic pairing; the herb helps improve the taste of tomatoes when grown together, and, of course, they're a match made in culinary heaven. Rosemary and beans share a mutual benefit relationship where rosemary's strong scent repels bean beetles, and its robust flavor infuses beans when cooked together. These pairings not only make sense in the garden but also inspire dishes that are bursting with freshness and flavor.

- Basil and tomatoes for taste improvement and culinary harmony.
- Rosemary with beans to repel pests and enhance flavor.

Herb Garden Companions

Creating a dedicated herb garden opens a realm of possibilities for companion planting within this aromatic world. Lavender, with its soothing fragrance, can serve as a central feature, attracting pollinators while repelling fleas and moths, creating a sanctuary for both people and plants. Surround it with sage, which benefits from the same dry conditions lavender thrives in, and parsley, which can help keep the lavender's base weed-free due to its dense growth. Incorporating chives, which bloom with purple flowers that bees love, can add to the garden's allure while protecting against aphids. This herbaceous companionship fosters a space where each plant not only contributes to the collective beauty but also supports the health and productivity of its neighbors.

- Center your herb garden with lavender for pollination and pest control.
- Surround lavender with sage and parsley for mutual soil and maintenance benefits.
- Add chives for their pollinator-attracting flowers and aphid-repelling abilities.

Planting herbs in your garden is akin to weaving a tapestry, where each thread enhances the pattern's overall beauty and integrity. Through their aromatic protection, soil improvement efforts, culinary pairings, and harmonious relationships within an herb garden, herbs offer a multifaceted approach to successful gardening. They remind us that the garden is not just a place of cultivation but a space where nature's intricate connections unfold, offering protection, nourishment, and delight in every leaf and blossom.

COMPANION FLOWERS FOR VEGETABLE GARDENS

In every vegetable garden, there's an opportunity to weave in the delicate textures and vibrant hues of flowers, creating a space that's as pleasing to the eye as it is to the palate. Beyond their aesthetic appeal, flowers can play a crucial role in enhancing vegetable growth, offering natural pest control solutions, and attracting a bevy of pollinators to the garden. This section explores the symbiotic relationship between flowers and vegetables, revealing how the right floral companions can turn a simple vegetable plot into a flourishing, productive oasis.

Beauty and Function

Integrating flowers into the vegetable garden brings a dual benefit: they add splashes of color, breaking the green monotony with their blossoms, and serve functional roles that support the health and productivity of vegetable crops. Flowers can act as a line of defense against pests, luring them away from valuable veggies or deterring them altogether with their scents. Additionally, they can improve the garden's overall health by attracting beneficial insects that contribute to pest control and pollination. For example, planting tall, bright sunflowers at the garden's edge not only draws the eye but also serves as a beacon for pollinators and a barrier against wind, protecting more delicate vegetable plants.

Edible Flowers

The garden-to-table movement gains an extra layer of flavor and color with the inclusion of edible flowers. These blooms not only add ornamental value to the garden but also bring a unique taste and aesthetic to culinary creations:

- *Nasturtiums*: With their peppery flavor, nasturtium flowers and leaves are fantastic in salads or as garnishes. They're also known for their ability to attract aphids away from veggies, serving as a trap crop.
- *Calendula*: Often used to add a golden hue to dishes, calendula petals have a slightly spicy taste and can help deter tomato hornworms when planted near tomato plants.
- *Borage*: Star-shaped borage flowers offer a mild cucumber flavor, perfect for refreshing drinks or salads. Borage is particularly good at attracting bees and enhancing pollination in the garden.

Incorporating these and other edible flowers into your vegetable garden not only enriches your dining experience but also contributes to a more vibrant and resilient garden ecosystem.

Pollinator Attraction

A garden buzzing with pollinators is a sign of health and vitality. Certain flowers have a special knack for drawing these essential visitors, ensuring that your vegetable plants get pollinated and set fruit successfully:

- *Lavender*: Beloved for its fragrance and purple spikes, lavender attracts bees and butterflies, making it an excellent companion for pollinator-dependent crops like squash and cucumbers.
- *Zinnias*: These colorful, long-blooming flowers are magnets for hummingbirds and butterflies. Planting zinnias around the garden encourages these pollinators to visit, boosting the pollination rates of nearby vegetable plants.
- *Cosmos*: With their daisy-like flowers and feathery foliage, the cosmos are particularly appealing to bees. Their easy-going nature makes them suitable companions for a wide range of vegetables, enhancing the garden's overall pollination.
- *Borage:* Known as a "bee's paradise," its star-shaped flowers are a reliable source of nectar, ensuring bees frequently visit, aiding in the pollination of surrounding crops.

Strategically placing these pollinator-friendly flowers throughout the vegetable garden ensures a steady stream of pollinators, vital for the successful fruiting of many vegetable crops.

Flower and Vegetable Pairings

Finding the perfect floral companion for your vegetables and herbs can significantly impact their growth, yield, and ability to fend off pests. Here are some pairings that have proven their worth in gardens across various climates:

- *Marigolds and Tomatoes:* The strong scent of marigolds repels nematodes and tomato hornworms, making them invaluable allies for tomato plants. Their bright blooms also add a cheerful dash of color to the tomato patch.
- *Sweet Alyssum and Broccoli:* The tiny, fragrant flowers of sweet alyssum attract beneficial insects that prey on common pests like aphids, which can plague broccoli plants. Its low-growing tendency makes it an ideal ground cover, suppressing weeds and maintaining soil moisture.
- *Chrysanthemums and Kale:* Chrysanthemums contain pyrethrin, a natural insecticide effective against a variety of pests. Planting them near kale can help deter leaf-eaters, ensuring your kale leaves stay pristine.
- *Chives and Apple Trees:* The sulfur compounds they release can help prevent apple scab, protecting your fruit harvest.
- Basil and Calendula: Planting calendula near basil can help repel pests that typically target basil, while the basil encourages stronger calendula growth.
- Tomatoes and Nasturtiums: Nasturtiums act as a trap crop for aphids, drawing them away from tomatoes. Plus, their vibrant blooms add a hint of color to your tomato patch.

Choosing flowers that complement and support your vegetable garden can transform it from a mere collection of plants into a cohesive, integrated ecosystem where every element thrives. By selecting the proper floral companions, you not only improve the beauty and efficiency of your garden but also contribute to a healthier, more sustainable gardening practice. Whether you're drawn to the utility of edible flowers, the pollinator-attracting power of certain blooms, or the pest-deterring properties of others, incorporating flowers into your vegetable garden is a step toward a more vibrant, fruitful gardening experience.

THE ROLE OF COVER CROPS

Stepping into the realm of cover crops, we uncover a layer of gardening that's as protective as it is productive. These unsung heroes of the plant world serve multiple roles, from safeguarding the soil against erosion to acting as green manure and even keeping those persistent weeds at bay. Their inclusion in a companion planting strategy is akin to adding a robust bassline to a melody, providing depth and support that enriches the entire garden's harmony.

Soil Protection

Imagine the soil as a fragile artifact, exposed to the elements and vulnerable to being washed or blown away. Cover crops act like a shield, covering the soil's surface with a living blanket. Through their growth, they help bind the soil, making it harder for wind and water to erode it away. During rainy seasons, instead of the soil being washed out, the roots of cover crops hold it firmly in place, ensuring that the fertile top layer remains intact and ready for the next planting cycle. This protection is invaluable, especially in off-seasons when the garden might otherwise lie bare and exposed.

Green Manure

In the cyclical story of a garden, every end is a new beginning. Cover crops, when turned back into the soil, become green manure, contributing organic matter and nutrients back into the earth. Leguminous cover crops, in particular, are stars in this role, fixing nitrogen in the soil, which becomes available to the next generation of plants. This process enriches the soil naturally, reducing or even eliminating the need for synthetic fertilizers. It's a sustainable way to maintain soil fertility, ensuring that the garden's soil is not just alive but teeming with the nutrients future plants will need to thrive.

Weed Suppression

Weeds are opportunists, taking advantage of any available space to set root. However, with cover crops in place, the real estate for weeds diminishes significantly. The dense growth of cover crops leaves little room for weeds to establish, acting as a natural barrier. This suppression is twofold; not only do cover crops physically crowd out weeds, but they also can outcompete them for resources like sunlight, water, and nutrients. The result is a significant reduction in the gardener's need to weed, freeing up more time to enjoy the garden rather than laboring over it.

Cover Crop Selection and Management

Choosing the right cover crops and managing them effectively is critical to reap their full benefits. The selection depends on several factors, including the garden's specific needs, the climate, and what you plan to grow next. Some popular choices include:

- *Clover:* Excellent for nitrogen-fixing and attracting beneficial insects.

- *Rye:* Known for its ability to suppress weeds and prevent soil erosion.
- *Buckwheat:* Quick to grow and suitable for attracting pollinators.

In managing cover crops, timing is crucial. They need to be cut down or turned into the soil at the right moment, usually just before they set seed, to prevent them from becoming weeds themselves. This timing varies among crops, so keeping an eye on their growth stage is essential. Additionally, integrating cover crops into a rotating planting scheme can maximize their benefits, ensuring that each area of the garden gets its turn under this protective and enriching cover.

Incorporating cover crops into a companion planting strategy weaves a layer of sustainability and protection into the fabric of the garden. It's an approach that acknowledges the importance of soil health in the broader ecosystem of the garden, ensuring that the land is not just used but nurtured and preserved for future planting seasons. Cover crops stand as guardians of the garden, silently working to protect, enrich, and sustain the soil, making it a fertile foundation for whatever comes next.

Wrapping this journey into the supportive role of cover crops within companion planting, we're reminded of the interconnectedness of all elements within the garden. From the smallest microorganism in the soil to the tallest sunflower reaching for the sky, each plays a part in creating a thriving, sustainable ecosystem. The use of cover crops embodies this interconnectedness, offering a bridge between seasons and a promise of fertility and protection for the soil that sustains all life in the garden. As we move forward, we carry with us the knowledge that nurturing the soil is as crucial as caring for the plants it supports, each contributing to the vibrant tapestry of life that makes up the garden.

5

GROW YOUR OWN FOOD: BUILD A SELF SUSTAINING GARDEN

IN THE PURSUIT of ecological harmony and sustainability, this chapter unveils the pathway toward establishing a self-sustaining garden that thrives with minimal human intervention yet produces abundantly. At the core of this green odyssey is the principle of permaculture, a design philosophy that not only mimics the patterns and relationships found in nature but also offers a multitude of benefits. By embracing permaculture, gardeners create ecosystems that conserve resources, enhance soil fertility, and sustain plant and animal species diversity, laying the foundation for a garden that nurtures itself and its caretakers.

A pivotal element in this sustainable symphony is the role of beneficial insects. These natural allies, such as bees for pollination and ladybugs for pest control, play a crucial role in reducing the need for toxic chemical pesticides and fertilizers. By attracting them, gardeners foster a healthier, more vibrant garden environment. This natural pest management not only supports plant health but also contributes to the biodiversity that is vital for ecological balance.

As we delve deeper, vertical planting emerges as an ingenious strategy to maximize space, allowing for greater yields and diversity within the garden. This method not only optimizes the use of vertical space but also improves air circulation and light exposure, which are essential for plant health and productivity. Additionally, vertical planting can create a visually appealing garden, adding to the overall aesthetic value of your space.

Lastly, the integration of aquaponics introduces a revolutionary approach to garden sustainability. This system combines aquaculture with hydroponics in a symbiotic environment where fish and plants support each other's growth. Aquaponics exemplifies the ultimate in self-sustaining gardening, recycling nutrients and water in a closed-loop system that is both efficient and environmentally friendly.

This chapter aims to guide you toward establishing a garden that thrives on the principles of sustainability and self-sufficiency, mirroring the intricate balance of natural ecosystems.

COMPANION PLANTING IN PERMACULTURE

Permaculture is a design philosophy that looks to mimic the no-waste, interdependent systems found in nature. It's a holistic approach to gardening and farming, aiming to create ecosystems that sustain themselves with minimal human intervention. When we talk about permaculture, companion planting plays a crucial role. It's not just about putting plants together for mutual benefit; it's about creating a thriving community where each element supports the others, much like relationships found in natural ecosystems.

Permaculture Principles

At the heart of permaculture are three core ethics: care for the earth, care for the people, and fair share. These principles guide the design process, influencing how companion plants are selected and arranged. The aim is to create systems that are sustainable and self-sufficient, reducing waste and energy input while increasing productivity. Companion planting in this context is about more than just plant interactions; it's about integrating plants, animals, and humans into a system where each element benefits the others.

- *Observation and Interaction:* Taking time to understand the natural processes and cycles in your garden allows for more informed decisions about which plants to pair together.
- *Catch and Store Energy:* Utilizing plants that can attract beneficial insects or provide shade can create microclimates or enhance soil fertility, effectively storing the energy of the ecosystem for future use.
- *Use and Value Diversity:* A diverse planting strategy ensures a more resilient and productive garden. Companion planting, when applied using permaculture principles,

embraces this diversity, creating a garden that is more resistant to pests and diseases.

Guild Planting

One of the most fascinating aspects of permaculture is the concept of plant guilds. A guild is a group of plants (and sometimes animals) that work together to create a micro-ecosystem where each member contributes to the whole. For example, a simple apple tree guild might include:

- Comfrey at the base, with its deep roots, brings up nutrients from the subsoil, making them available to the shallower-rooted companions.
- Daffodils are planted around the drip line to deter apple borers and other pests.
- Clover as a ground cover, fixing nitrogen in the soil and giving it a habitat for beneficial insects.

Each plant in the guild supports the others, either by providing nutrients, offering protection from pests, or attracting pollinators. This interdependence results in a healthier, more productive garden with less need for external inputs.

Design Considerations

When integrating companion planting into permaculture systems, several design considerations come into play. Layering and zoning are two key concepts:

- *Layering:* This involves creating a vertical stack of different plants, each occupying a different layer in the garden, from

tall trees at the top to root crops underground. This maximizes space and mimics natural forest systems.
- *Zoning:* Plants are arranged based on how often they need human attention. Herbs and salad greens might be placed in zone 1, close to the house, while fruit trees and other low-maintenance plants occupy further zones.

Both of these design strategies aim to create a garden that is efficient, productive, and easy to manage by placing plants in positions where they can most effectively support each other and the ecosystem as a whole.

Case Studies

Seeing permaculture and companion planting in action can provide valuable insights. Here are a couple of real-world examples:

- *A Suburban Permaculture Garden:* In a suburb, a family transformed their backyard into a thriving permaculture garden. By planting a variety of fruit trees, vegetables, herbs, and flowers together, they created a system that requires minimal watering and no chemical fertilizers. The garden now produces a significant portion of their food year-round.
- *An Urban Permaculture Project:* In a densely populated city, a community came together to turn a vacant lot into a permaculture garden. Using companion planting and guilds, they were able to harvest a wide array of crops in a small space. The garden has become a source of fresh produce for the community and a habitat for urban wildlife.

These examples show that, with thoughtful design and an understanding of ecological principles, it's possible to create gardens that are not only productive and sustainable but also beautiful and harmonious. Each plant, insect, and human participant in the garden contributes to a system that is greater than the sum of its parts, embodying the essence of permaculture and the power of companion planting.

ATTRACTING BENEFICIAL INSECTS

Gardens are bustling ecosystems, home not just to plants but a host of insects that play pivotal roles in the health and productivity of your garden. Among these, beneficial insects are the unsung heroes, tirelessly working to control pests and pollinate plants. Understanding how to invite these allies into your garden is vital to a balanced, thriving ecosystem.

Identifying Allies

Several insects are crucial for keeping pest populations in check and ensuring your plants stay healthy:

- *Ladybugs:* These beetles are voracious aphid eaters, capable of consuming up to 50 aphids a day.
- *Lacewings:* Both adult lacewings and their larvae feed on a wide variety of pests, such as aphids, mites, and caterpillar eggs.
- *Hoverflies:* The larvae of these flies are effective against aphids, while the adults help with pollination.
- *Ground Beetles:* These beetles are night-time hunters, preying on slugs, snails, and other ground-dwelling pests.

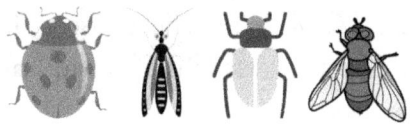

Attracting these beneficial insects involves understanding what they need for survival—food, water, and shelter—and incorporating elements that meet these needs into your garden design.

Insectary Plants

Integrating insectary plants—those that specifically attract beneficial insects—into your garden is an effective way to bolster your garden's defense system. These plants can be easily woven into your companion planting strategy:

- *Fennel and Dill:* Attract a wide range of beneficial insects, including ladybugs and lacewings, with their flowers.
- *Yarrow:* Its clusters of small flowers are irresistible to many beneficial insects, offering both a feeding and nesting site.
- *Sweet Alyssum:* The sweet fragrance of its flowers attracts hoverflies and parasitic wasps, both of which control pest populations.

Incorporating a variety of these plants not only supports a robust community of beneficial insects but also adds to the garden's aesthetic appeal.

Creating Habitats

Creating inviting habitats for beneficial insects means they're more likely to stay in your garden, offering their pest control services throughout the season. Here are some strategies to make your garden more insect-friendly:

- *Leave some bare soil:* Many beneficial insects, including certain bees and beetles, nest in the ground and require access to undisturbed soil.
- *Provide water sources:* A shallow dish filled with stones and water offers a safe place for insects to drink without the risk of drowning.
- *Offer shelter:* Piles of leaves, brush, or even specially designed insect hotels provide necessary shelter for many beneficial insects to nest and overwinter.

Ensuring your garden caters to the basic needs of these insects transforms it into a welcoming haven for them.

Monitoring and Maintenance

Keeping an eye on the insect populations in your garden allows you to gauge the health of your ecosystem and make adjustments as necessary. Regularly inspect your plants for both pests and beneficial insects, taking note of any changes:

- *Early morning is best:* Many insects are more active in the cooler morning hours, making it easier to spot them.
- *Keep a garden journal:* Record your observations, including which plants are attracting certain insects, to guide future garden planning.
- *Adjust as needed:* If you notice an imbalance—too many pests and not enough beneficial insects—consider introducing more insectary plants or habitats to tip the scales back in favor of your garden's defenders.

A proactive way to monitor and maintain your garden's insect population ensures a dynamic, balanced ecosystem where plants and insects support each other in mutual benefit.

By inviting beneficial insects into your garden and providing for their needs, you create a natural, self-regulating system that reduces the need for chemical interventions, promotes biodiversity, and contributes to the overall health of your garden. This approach, grounded in the understanding of the garden as an interconnected ecosystem, leads to a more resilient, productive, and visually stunning garden space.

VERTICAL COMPANION PLANTING

In the realm of small-space gardening, the sky truly is the limit. With a bit of creativity and strategic planning, vertical companion planting allows gardeners to expand upwards, transforming even the tiniest of spaces into lush, productive havens. This approach not only maximizes the use of available space but also introduces a dynamic layer of beauty and biodiversity to your garden.

Maximizing Space

The concept of vertical companion planting hinges on the efficient use of vertical space to enhance garden productivity. This method is particularly beneficial in urban settings or small backyards, where horizontal space is at a premium. By directing plant growth upwards, gardeners can significantly increase their growing area, allowing for a wider variety of plants in a compact space. This technique also improves air circulation around plants, reducing the risk of fungal diseases, and can make garden maintenance tasks like watering and harvesting more accessible.

Support Structures

The backbone of any vertical garden is its supporting structures, which can vary widely in material, design, and complexity. Here are a few ideas:

- *Trellises:* Simple lattice or wire trellises can support a variety of climbing plants, from beans to cucumbers, and can be easily attached to walls or fences.
- *Stakes and Poles:* For taller crops like tomatoes, sturdy stakes or poles provide the necessary support, keeping plants upright and productive.
- *Towers:* Vertical towers or garden columns offer an all-in-one solution for growing multiple plants in a single, space-saving unit. They're especially great for herbs and strawberries.
- *Hanging Baskets:* Perfect for trailing plants, hanging baskets can be suspended from balconies, decks, or sturdy branches, adding a vertical element without the need for ground space.

When choosing support structures, consider the weight they'll need to support and ensure they're securely anchored to withstand the elements and the growing weight of maturing plants.

Plant Selection

Choosing the right plants for vertical companion planting is crucial. Not only should the selected plants be suited for vertical growth, but they also need to be compatible companions, sharing similar light and water requirements. Here are some guidelines:

- *Weight Considerations:* Ensure the chosen plants won't exceed the weight capacity of your support structures. Lightweight climbers like peas are suitable for most trellises, while heavier fruits like melons may require more robust support.
- *Growth Habit:* Opt for plants with natural climbing tendencies or those that can be easily trained to grow upwards. Pole beans, vine tomatoes, and cucumbers are excellent choices.
- *Light Requirements:* Place taller plants on the north side of the structure to prevent them from casting shade on shorter companions, ensuring all plants receive adequate sunlight.

By carefully selecting plants based on these criteria, you can create a harmonious vertical garden that thrives.

Vertical Pairing Examples

Creating successful vertical companion plantings involves more than just stacking plants vertically; it's about fostering mutually beneficial relationships between them. Here are a few pairings that exemplify the potential of this approach:

- *Climbing Roses and Clematis:* This classic floral duo brings together the structural beauty of roses with the climbing vigor of clematis, resulting in a stunning display that

maximizes vertical space. The clematis benefits from the shade provided by the rose's foliage, while both plants enjoy improved air circulation and less competition for root space.
- *Squash and Corn:* An adaptation of the traditional Three Sisters planting, with squash vines trained to climb cornstalks. The squash leaves provide ground cover, conserving moisture for both plants, while the cornstalks offer a natural trellis for the squash vines.
- *Tomatoes and Basil:* When grown in vertical containers, tomatoes benefit from the proximity to basil, which can assist in repelling pests like flies and mosquitoes. This pairing also makes efficient use of vertical space, with basil filling in the lower tier of the container garden.
- *Strawberries and Thyme:* In a vertical planting system, strawberries can be positioned to cascade over the sides, while thyme, planted at the top, trails down among the strawberry plants. Thyme's aromatic oils help deter pests from the strawberries, and its drought tolerance makes it a low-maintenance companion.

Each of these pairings takes into account the unique needs and benefits of the plants involved, creating a symbiotic relationship that enhances the health, beauty, and productivity of the garden. By thoughtfully integrating vertical companion planting into your garden design, you can unlock new dimensions of gardening success, turning vertical space into a verdant, flourishing canvas.

COMPANION PLANTING WITH AQUAPONICS

In the realm of sustainable gardening, aquaponics emerges as a shining beacon of innovation, intertwining the growth of plants and aquatic animals in a dance of mutual benefit. This eco-friendly approach harnesses the natural symbiosis between fish and plants, creating a closed-loop ecosystem that mimics the interconnectedness found in natural ecosystems. Here, fish waste provides an organic nutrient source for the plants, while the plants, in turn, help filter and purify the water, which is then routed back to the fish. This seamless integration not only conserves water but also eliminates the need for chemical fertilizers, embodying the principles of sustainability and efficiency.

System Basics

At its core, an aquaponics system is a blend of aquaculture (raising fish) and hydroponics (growing plants in water without soil). The system operates on a simple yet profound principle: fish produce waste containing ammonia, which, through natural processes, is converted by beneficial bacteria into nitrates—a form of nitrogen that plants can absorb and use to grow. This cycle of life, conversion, and growth unfolds within the system, offering a fascinating glimpse into the efficiency of nature's design.

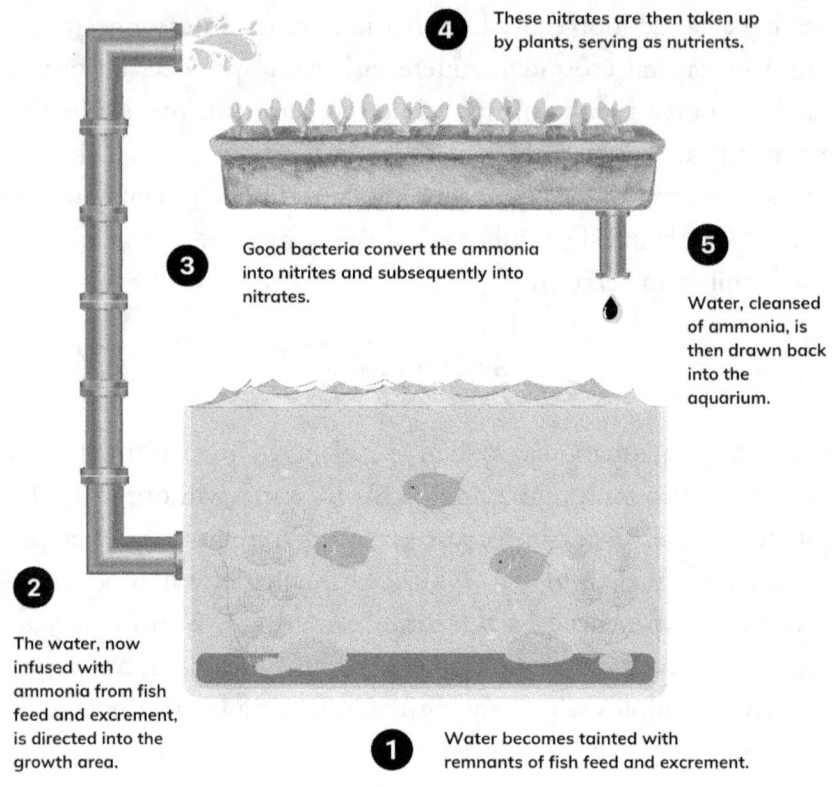

Water Quality Benefits

One of the most compelling aspects of aquaponics is its contribution to maintaining high-quality water for both plants and fish. The plants act as an organic filter, absorbing the nitrates and other nutrients from the water, which could build up to toxic levels for the fish. This process not only ensures the health and well-being of the aquatic animals but also promotes vigorous plant growth, all while conserving water by recirculating it within the system. Moreover, the constant movement of water helps to keep the root systems of plants oxygenated, further enhancing their growth and productivity.

Plant and Fish Pairings

Navigating the world of aquaponics involves selecting plant and fish combinations that thrive together, creating a balanced ecosystem. Here are some guidelines for crafting successful pairings:

- Leafy Greens and Tilapia: Hardy and adaptable, tilapia is an excellent choice for beginners. Paired with nutrient-loving leafy greens such as lettuce, kale, and spinach, this combination can yield abundant harvests.
- Herbs and Goldfish: For smaller systems, goldfish can be a low-maintenance option. Pair them with herbs like basil, mint, and cilantro, which thrive in nutrient-rich water, adding flavor and variety to your garden.
- Tomatoes and Carp: Carp, including koi, are robust fish that produce a significant amount of waste, making them suitable for supporting fruiting plants like tomatoes, peppers, and cucumbers, which have higher nutrient demands.

Achieving harmony in an aquaponics system means balancing the nutrient production of the fish with the nutrient demands of the plants, ensuring both can thrive without overburdening the system.

Maintenance and Monitoring

Keeping your aquaponics system in peak condition requires regular maintenance and monitoring, focusing on water chemistry, plant health, and fish welfare:

- *Water Chemistry:* Regular testing of pH, ammonia, nitrite, and nitrate levels is crucial to prevent toxic buildup and ensure the system remains balanced. You should aim for a

pH level between 6.8 and 7.2 for optimal plant and fish health.
- *Plant Health:* Watch for signs of nutrient deficiencies in plants, which may indicate the need to adjust feeding rates or fish populations. Healthy plants should exhibit vibrant growth and color.
- *Fish Welfare:* Monitor fish for signs of stress or disease, maintaining appropriate stocking densities and feeding practices to keep them healthy and happy.

Routine checks and adjustments ensure the system functions smoothly, providing a sustainable source of fresh produce and fish, all within the confines of your own backyard or indoor space.

After looking at companion planting with aquaponics, it's clear that this innovative approach offers more than just a method of food production. It represents a step toward a more sustainable and harmonious way of living, where the principles of mutual benefit and interdependence are not just observed but actively practiced. Through aquaponics, we glimpse the potential for a future where our food systems work with nature rather than against it, embodying the ideals of efficiency, sustainability, and balance. As we move forward, let this chapter serve as a reminder of the transformative power of integrating principles of companion planting into modern gardening practices, paving the way for a greener, more bountiful world.

6

ROOT WISDOM: NURTURING YOUR GARDENS

PICTURE the early morning in a garden, dew still clinging to the leaves, the air fresh and cool. This is nature's way of watering, gentle and efficient, nurturing every root with just what it needs to thrive. In our own gardens, achieving this level of harmony with water can seem like a lofty goal. Yet, with a bit of insight and the proper techniques, we can come close to creating environments where our plants not only survive but flourish together. This chapter dives into the various methods available to cater to the unique needs of companion-planted gardens.

Efficient Watering Practices

When it comes to watering, more isn't always better. The secret lies in precision—getting water directly to where it's most needed: the roots. Two methods stand out for their efficiency:

- *Drip Irrigation:* Imagine a slow, steady trickle of water delivered directly to the base of each plant. This not only conserves water but also keeps the leaves dry, reducing the risk of disease. Creating a drip irrigation system can be as simple as laying a hose with tiny holes along your garden beds, ensuring each plant gets a sip directly at its roots.
- *Soaker Hoses:* Similar to drip irrigation, soaker hoses lay on the soil surface but release water along their entire length. They're perfect for long rows of plants, soaking the soil slowly so water penetrates deeply, encouraging strong root growth.

Both methods minimize waste and ensure water goes precisely where it's needed, making them ideal for the diverse needs of a companion-planted garden.

Watering Schedule Optimization

Creating a watering schedule that fits the unique tapestry of a companion garden means observing and adjusting. Here's how to get started:

- *Morning is Prime Time:* Watering in the early hours mimics nature's dew, allowing water to seep deep into the soil before the sun's heat increases evaporation. It also helps keep plant leaves dry throughout the day, discouraging fungal diseases.
- *Watch the Weather:* Let nature lend a hand. Rainy days mean a break from watering but always double-check the soil moisture to ensure your plants are getting what they need.
- *Group by Thirst:* Plant companions with similar water needs together. This strategy simplifies your watering schedule and ensures that each plant community receives the right amount of moisture.

Understanding Plant Needs

Each plant in your companion garden has its own unique thirst. Tuning into these needs prevents both underwatering and overwatering, which can stress plants and lead to poor growth or disease. Here's a strategy for getting to know your garden's water needs:

- *Check the Soil:* Before reaching for the hose, dig a finger into the soil near your plants. If the soil is dry an inch or two below the surface, it's time to water. If it's still moist, you can wait.
- *Observe Plant Signals:* Wilting leaves can indicate thirst, but check the soil to confirm. Sometimes, plants wilt in the heat of the day, only to perk up in the evening. This doesn't always signal a need for water.
- *Use a Moisture Meter:* For a more scientific approach, a simple moisture meter can take the guesswork out of when to water, giving you a clear read on soil moisture levels around different plants.

Mulch as a Moisture Regulator

Mulch isn't just about making your garden look tidy. It's a key player in maintaining soil moisture, acting much like a blanket that keeps the soil cool and moist. Here are some tips to use mulch effectively:

- *Choose Organic Mulches:* Straw, bark, or shredded leaves not only retain moisture but also help break down over time, enriching the soil.
- *Apply the Right Amount:* A layer of 2-3 inches is usually enough to conserve moisture without suffocating plant roots. Be sure to leave a little space around the base of each plant to prevent rot.
- *Refresh as Needed:* Over time, mulch breaks down or may be washed away. Check your mulch layer periodically and add more as needed to ensure ongoing moisture retention and soil protection.

Incorporating these watering strategies into your companion gardening can transform the task from guesswork into a mindful practice. By observing the needs of your plants, choosing efficient watering methods, and using mulch to regulate soil moisture, you create a garden ecosystem that's resilient, productive, and deeply connected to the rhythms of nature. This approach not only saves water and time but also nurtures your garden's roots, fostering a vibrant community of plants that grow stronger together.

MULCHING TYPES & TECHNIQUES

Mulching is the equivalent of giving your garden a cozy blanket, one that not only keeps it warm but also wards off unwanted guests like weeds and ensures it stays hydrated. Understanding the different types of mulch and how to apply them can transform your companion garden into a more resilient and self-sufficient system. It's a simple yet profoundly impactful way to care for your plants.

Types of Mulch

In the universe of mulching materials, two main categories emerge: organic and inorganic. Each has its unique set of benefits and uses within a companion planting framework.

- Organic Mulches include materials like straw, wood chips, leaves, and grass clippings. These materials break down over time, enrich the soil with nutrients, and improve its structure. This makes organic mulches a fantastic choice for companion gardens, where soil health is vital to plant synergy. Straw, for example, is light and easy to spread around delicate stems, making it ideal for mulching between closely planted companions.
- Inorganic Mulches, such as rocks, gravel, and landscape fabric, don't provide nutrients to the soil since they don't decompose. However, they excel in weed suppression and moisture retention over more extended periods. Pebbles can be particularly useful around heat-loving plants, reflecting

light and conserving heat to extend the growing season.

Application Methods

Applying mulch correctly ensures your plants reap maximum benefits. Here's a step-by-step guide to mulching your companion garden:

- *Prepare the Area:* Before laying mulch, remove weeds and water the soil thoroughly. This creates a clean slate and ensures the soil is moist under the mulch.
- *Spread Evenly:* Using your hands or a gardening tool, spread the mulch around your plants, aiming for an even layer approximately 2-3 inches thick. Be mindful to leave some breathing room around the base of each plant to prevent a buildup of moisture and potential rot.
- *Water Lightly:* After mulching, a light watering helps settle the mulch into place, ensuring it starts working to retain moisture right away.

Mulch and Pest Control

Mulch does more than just insulate the soil and retain moisture; it plays a strategic role in pest management. Certain organic mulches can deter pests:

- Cedar and Pine Bark Chips are known for their pest-repelling qualities. Their natural oils can deter certain insects, making them an excellent choice for companion plants that are susceptible to pest invasions.
- Straw Mulch can create a habitat for spiders and ground beetles, natural predators that help keep pest populations in check.

Incorporating these mulches into your garden contributes to a holistic pest management strategy, reducing the need for chemical interventions.

Seasonal Mulching

Adapting your mulching practices to the seasons ensures your garden remains protected and productive year-round:

- *Spring:* A lighter layer of mulch in spring helps the soil warm up more quickly, encouraging earlier growth. It's also the perfect time to introduce mulch around heat-loving companion plants, preparing them for the growing season.
- *Summer:* This is when mulch shows its true colors, conserving moisture and keeping roots cool. Refresh mulch layers as needed to maintain adequate coverage and moisture retention.
- *Fall:* Applying a thicker layer of mulch in fall can protect soil and plant roots from the impending cold, while decomposing organic mulch adds nutrients back to the soil, prepping it for the next growing season.
- *Winter:* In colder climates, mulch acts as an insulator, protecting perennials and overwintering crops from freeze-thaw cycles that can heave and damage roots.

Adjusting your mulching technique with the changing seasons not only safeguards your plants but also promotes a thriving garden ecosystem throughout the year.

NATURAL FERTILIZERS FOR A HEALTHY GARDEN

In the tapestry of companion planting, the role of fertilizers is akin to providing a balanced diet for your plants, ensuring they grow robust and resilient. Moving away from synthetic options, organic fertilizers emerge as the heroes of the garden, enriching the soil with life-sustaining nutrients while safeguarding the environment and our health.

Organic versus Synthetic Fertilizers

Organic fertilizers, made from natural sources like plants, animals, and minerals, offer a buffet of benefits that synthetic counterparts struggle to match. They release nutrients at a slower, more consistent rate, mirroring the natural growth rhythm of plants. This gradual nourishment fosters stronger root systems and enhances soil structure by encouraging the proliferation of beneficial microbes. These microbes not only break down organic matter into vital nutrients but also improve soil aeration and water retention. Unlike synthetic fertilizers, which can degrade soil health over time, organic options build it up, creating a fertile foundation for your companion garden to thrive.

DIY Fertilizer Recipes

Crafting your own natural fertilizers not only cuts down on costs but also recycles kitchen and garden waste, turning it into gold for your garden. Here are a few recipes to get you started:

- *Compost Tea:* Steep fully matured compost in water for a few days, stirring occasionally. Strain and use this nutrient-rich liquid to water your plants, providing them with a gentle dose of essential nutrients.
- *Eggshell and Coffee Ground Fertilizer:* Dry and crush eggshells; then mix with used coffee grounds. Sprinkle this mixture around your plants. The calcium from eggshells aids in cell growth, while coffee grounds add nitrogen to the soil, stimulating plant growth.
- *Banana Peel Potion:* Soak banana peels in water for a couple of days. Use the infused water for plants craving potassium, like tomatoes and peppers. This boosts flowering and fruiting, leading to a bountiful harvest.

Application Timing and Techniques

Timing and technique are critical when applying organic fertilizers to ensure plants receive the maximum benefit without harm. Here's how to navigate this:

- *Seasonal Timing:* Apply fertilizers when plants are most active. Early spring is ideal for giving plants a boost at the start of their growing season. A mid-season top-up can support continued growth and productivity.
- *Method of Application:* For solid fertilizers like compost, spread evenly around the base of plants, gently adding it into the top layer of soil without disturbing the roots. Liquid fertilizers, such as compost tea, can be added directly on the soil or used as a foliar spray for a quick nutrient

boost.
- *Mind the Quantity:* Over-fertilizing can lead to nutrient burn, harming the plants. Follow the less-is-more principle, observing plant response and adjusting as necessary.

Fertilizers and Plant Compatibility

Different companion plant pairings have unique nutritional needs. Tailoring your fertilization approach to these needs can enhance the harmony and productivity of your garden:

- *Heavy Feeders and Light Feeders:* Plant heavy feeders, such as tomatoes and corn, alongside light feeders, like herbs and onions. Amend the soil with a rich compost for the heavy feeders while sparing the light feeders, which thrive in less fertile soil.
- *Nitrogen-Loving and Nitrogen-Fixing Pairs:* Pair nitrogen-loving plants like leafy greens with nitrogen-fixing legumes. The legumes enrich the soil with nitrogen, benefiting their companions. A light application of a nitrogen-rich fertilizer can boost this effect without overwhelming the legumes.
- *pH Preferences:* Some companion pairs, like blueberries (acid-loving) and strawberries (slightly acid to neutral), have different pH preferences. Customizing your fertilization strategy, such as using sulfur to lower the pH of blueberries, can cater to these needs without disrupting the balance.

In the vibrant world of companion planting, where diversity reigns, understanding and applying natural fertilizers with mindfulness can turn your garden into a thriving ecosystem. This approach nourishes not just the plants but the soil and the myriad of life it supports, reinforcing the cycle of growth and abundance that characterizes a truly healthy garden. By choosing organic fertilizers, crafting your own blends, applying them with care, and tailoring them to the specific needs of your plant companions, you empower your garden to reach its full potential, season after season.

PRUNING & HARVESTING

In the lush, intertwined world of companion planting, the acts of pruning and harvesting are not merely chores but rather essential rituals that sustain and invigorate our gardens. These practices, when executed with care and understanding, can significantly enhance the health, yield, and beauty of our companion-planted beds. In this section, we'll explore the nuanced art of pruning for vitality and harvesting for abundance, ensuring that each plant contributes its best to the collective symphony of the garden.

Pruning for Health and Yield

Pruning, the selective removal of plant parts, is vital for encouraging a garden that's not just surviving but thriving. It's about creating space for light and air to reach every leaf and bud, ensuring that plants direct their energy towards producing robust blooms and bountiful yields.

- *Selective Thinning:* In densely planted beds, selectively remove overcrowded stems or branches. This action prevents the spread of diseases that thrive in damp, airless conditions and ensures that remaining stems receive more sunlight and airflow.
- *Promoting Fruitful Growth:* For plants like tomatoes and peppers, removing some of the non-fruiting branches can redirect the plant's energy towards developing larger, healthier fruits. Snip off the "suckers" or side shoots that appear in the joints of tomato plants to focus growth on the main fruit-bearing stems.
- *Height Control:* For taller plants, such as certain beans that might overshadow their companions, trimming the tops once they reach a desired height can prevent them from monopolizing sunlight and allows for the lower-growing plants to have their share of the rays.

Harvesting Tips for Continuous Production

Harvesting is not just the rewarding end of the growing cycle; it's also a strategic tool for encouraging plants to produce more. Here's how to harvest with an eye toward inspiring continued growth and productivity:

- *Selective Picking:* Harvest vegetables and fruits as they ripen. Removing the mature crops signals the plant to keep producing. This method works wonders with beans, peas, and tomatoes.
- *Cut-and-Come-Again:* Many leafy greens, such as lettuce and kale, can be harvested leaf by leaf rather than taking the whole plant. Snip or pinch off the outer leaves and watch the plant continue to produce new ones from the center. This approach can extend the harvest period significantly.

- *Regular Berry Collection:* For berry plants, frequent harvesting encourages the plant to produce more fruit. Berries like strawberries and raspberries will yield more fruit the more often they are picked.

Managing Overgrowth

In the vibrant dance of a companion garden, plants can sometimes step on each other's toes, metaphorically speaking. Managing overgrowth ensures that all plants have the space and resources they need to flourish:

- *Maintaining Boundaries:* Vigorous growers, such as mint or certain types of squash, can quickly encroach on their neighbors' space. Regular trimming of these enthusiastic spreaders helps maintain balance in the garden, ensuring each plant has room to grow.
- *Vertical Training:* Utilize trellises, stakes, or cages to guide vines and tall plants upward rather than letting them sprawl across the ground. This not only saves space but also reduces the risk of disease by improving air circulation around the plants.

Seasonal Pruning and Care

As the seasons turn, our gardens ask different things of us. Adapting our care routines to these cycles can help prepare our plants for the transitions, ensuring they remain vigorous and productive:

- *Spring Preparation:* Early in the growing season, prune fruit trees and bushes to shape them and remove any dead or diseased wood. This cleanup encourages healthier, more productive growth. For perennials, trim back last year's

growth to make way for fresh shoots.
- *Summer Maintenance:* Throughout the growing season, keep an eye out for and remove any diseased or damaged foliage. This not only improves the appearance of your garden but also minimizes the spread of pests and diseases.
- *Autumn Wind-Down:* As the growing season comes to a close, reduce pruning activities to allow plants to prepare for dormancy. However, removing dead annuals and cleaning up debris can help prevent overwintering pests and diseases.
- *Winter Readiness:* In climates where winters are harsh, some perennials may benefit from a protective layer of mulch after the ground freezes. However, avoid heavy pruning at this time, as cuts may not heal before the cold sets in, leaving plants vulnerable.

MANAGING PESTS NATURALLY

In a garden where companionship between plants forms the root of its vitality, the presence of pests poses a delicate challenge. The balance between warding off unwanted visitors while rolling out the welcome mat for helpful critters is a dance every gardener learns over time. This part of our garden journey shines a light on recognizing allies among insects, employing nature-inspired pest control tactics, and the strategic placement of plants for a harmonious garden ecosystem.

Identifying Beneficial versus Harmful Insects

First, understanding who's who in the insect world is crucial. Beneficial insects like ladybugs, lacewings, and some types of wasps are nature's pest control agents. They feast on the insects that harm our plants, like aphids, mites, and caterpillars. On the flip side, recognizing pests is equally important. Telltale signs include visible damage to leaves, stems, or fruits and the actual sighting of the culprits. One way to encourage beneficial insects is to plant flowers they're attracted to, such as marigolds or cosmos, which can act as natural lures, keeping them close to the plants they protect.

Natural Pest Control Solutions

When pests do invade, reaching for chemical solutions isn't our only option. Nature provides several effective remedies:

- *Neem Oil:* A natural pesticide, neem oil works wonders in deterring a wide range of garden pests. Its application on affected plants can stop pests in their tracks without harming beneficial insects when used as directed.
- *Diatomaceous Earth:* This powder substance is made from fossilized algae, and it is a non-toxic pest deterrent. Sprinkling it around the base of plants can protect them from crawling pests like slugs and beetles.
- *Homemade Sprays:* A simple spray made from diluted soap and water can help manage soft-bodied pests like aphids and spider mites. For a stronger solution, blending garlic or chili peppers with water and a drop of soap creates a spray that pests find particularly repulsive.

Interplanting for Pest Management

The strategic placement of certain plants next to each other can naturally reduce pest invasions. This method, known as interplanting, uses the natural properties of plants to repel pests:

- Planting garlic among roses can deter aphids, which are notoriously attracted to roses but repelled by garlic's strong

scent.
- Growing chives near apple trees can help prevent apple scab, a common fungal issue, thanks to the sulfur compounds released by chives.
- Basil, when planted near tomatoes, not only improves their flavor but also repels flies and mosquitoes.

These pairings illustrate how companion planting can serve as a form of pest management, reducing the need for external interventions.

Monitoring and Response

Keeping a close eye on your garden allows for early detection of pest issues, making them easier to manage before they become widespread. Regular checks, especially during the peak growing season, can reveal the onset of problems. When pests are spotted, rapid response is critical. Remove them by hand where possible or apply one of the natural remedies mentioned. For diseases, removing and destroying affected plant parts can prevent the spread to healthy foliage.

At times, despite our best efforts, pests can get the upper hand. In such cases, understanding when to accept a level of damage as part of the natural ebb and flow of the garden ecosystem is essential. Often, a slight pest presence won't significantly harm overall plant health or yield.

In wrapping up, this exploration into natural pest management within companion planting underscores the beauty and intricacy of creating a garden in balance with nature. By learning to identify and encourage beneficial insects, employing natural remedies for pest control, and strategically placing plants to support each other, we cultivate not only a garden that's resilient and productive but also one that thrives in harmony with the ecosystem surrounding it. As we move forward, these principles of mindfulness and balance in our approach to pest management will continue to guide us, ensuring our gardens remain places of both abundance and ecological integrity.

7

SPRING INTO GARDENING: A FRESH START FOR COMPANION PLANTING

When the frost retreats and the days stretch longer, the garden stirs from its winter slumber, beckoning for a new cycle of life to begin. Spring, with its promise of renewal, offers a canvas that is fresh and ready for the vibrant strokes of companion plants.

This season sets the stage for the unfolding drama of growth, where each plant, a character in its own right, plays a role in a meticulously crafted plot of mutual support and flourishing harmony. It's in these early days that the foundation for a productive year is laid through thoughtful preparation, strategic pairings, and vigilant care against the unpredictability of spring weather.

Preparing Beds and Containers

Before seeds touch the soil, ensuring your garden beds and containers are primed for planting is crucial. Here's how to get started:

- *Soil Amendment:* Spring is the perfect time to enrich your garden's soil. Incorporating compost or well-rotted manure improves soil structure and fertility, creating an ideal environment for young plants to thrive. For container gardens, consider a fresh mix of potting soil enriched with compost to provide a nutrient-rich start.
- *Layout Planning:* Sketch out your garden layout, keeping companion planting principles in mind. Placing taller plants northward prevents them from casting shade on their shorter companions. Also, consider access for watering and harvesting—ensure paths allow you to reach every plant without stepping on others.

A neat trick is to use string and stakes to outline planting zones within your beds, a visual guide that helps in organizing space efficiently.

Early Season Companion Planting

Some plants are more eager than others to greet the spring sun. These early risers can be paired for mutual benefit, even when the air still holds a chill:

- *Peas and Carrots:* Peas, loving the cooler weather, can climb up trellises, leaving ground space for carrots, which appreciate the pea plants' shade in the warmer days to come.
- *Lettuce and Radishes:* Fast-growing radishes can mark the rows for slower-germinating lettuce, providing a quick harvest while lettuce matures. The radishes' leaves also offer a modest canopy, keeping lettuce cool.

Remember, the key to successful early companion planting is choosing pairings that share similar light and moisture needs but don't compete for space or nutrients.

Frost Protection Strategies

Even the most carefully planned garden can face the setback of a late frost. Protecting your tender seedlings is paramount:

- *Cloches and Row Covers:* Simple, transparent cloches, or floating row covers, can shield individual plants or entire rows from frost. These can be easily lifted during the day to allow for sunlight and air circulation.
- *Mulching:* A layer of organic mulch will help insulate the soil, keeping root systems warm. Straw or leaf mulch is ideal, as it can be pulled back easily on warmer days.

Always check the weather forecast. Preparing to cover your plants or even bringing containers indoors can save your spring garden from unexpected frost.

Spring Pest and Disease Watch

With new growth comes the attention of pests and diseases eager to take advantage of your garden's bounty:

- *Aphids:* These tiny pests can be managed early on by introducing ladybugs to your garden or spraying infested plants with a mixture of water and a few drops of dish soap.
- *Slugs and Snails:* These critters enjoy young seedlings. Surrounding your beds with a barrier of eggshells or diatomaceous earth can deter them.
- *Powdery Mildew:* This fungus favors cool, damp conditions. To prevent it, ensure good air circulation around your plants and consider a homemade spray of milk and water (1 part milk to 9 parts water).

Staying vigilant and responding quickly to any signs of pests or disease can help keep your garden healthy and productive.

Spring in the companion garden is a time of anticipation and preparation. It's when the groundwork is laid for a season of growth, beauty, and harvest. From enriching the soil in your beds and containers to choosing the correct plant pairs that will support each other in the coming months, every step taken is a step toward a flourishing garden. As the last threat of frost passes, being ready to protect your tender seedlings can make all the difference in getting your garden off to a strong start. With pests and diseases on the lookout for fresh growth, your early vigilance ensures that your plants can grow up strong and healthy, ready to face the warmer months ahead.

SUMMER MAINTENANCE TIPS

As the summer sun climbs high and the days stretch out in warmth, our gardens enter a period of rapid growth and vibrant life. This season, while bountiful, brings its own set of challenges and demands a shift in our care strategies to keep our companion plants thriving under the scorching sun.

Watering Adjustments

During the heat of summer, our garden's thirst escalates. The key to meeting this increased demand without wasting water or drowning our plants lies in smart watering tactics.

- *Early Morning Watering:* Water in the early morning. This timing allows water to seep deeply into the soil, reaching the roots where it's most needed before the heat of the day can cause surface evaporation.
- *Drip Systems and Soaker Hoses:* These tools become invaluable allies in summer. They deliver water straight to the base of the plant, minimizing loss and ensuring each drop serves its purpose. For companion-planted gardens, these systems can be adjusted to target specific zones, accommodating the varying needs of closely situated plants.
- *Check Soil Moisture Regularly:* Use a simple finger test or a soil moisture meter to gauge when your garden truly needs watering. Overwatering them can be just as bad as underwatering them, leading to root rot and other issues.

Mulching for Summer

As the season warms, mulch plays a starring role in conserving moisture and shielding the soil from the sun's intensity.

- *Organic Mulches:* Refresh your layer of organic mulch, such as straw or shredded bark, to about 2-3 inches thick. This layer acts like a natural insulator, keeping the soil cool and moist longer.
- *Mulch Placement:* Spread the mulch carefully around your plants, ensuring a uniform layer that covers the soil yet leaves some space around the stem bases to prevent rot and encourage air circulation.
- *Mulch Types:* While organic mulches are beneficial for their soil-enhancing properties, in some cases, inorganic mulches like pebbles can be used around heat-loving plants to reflect light and conserve heat, promoting growth.

Summer Pruning

Pruning in the summer has multiple benefits, from encouraging fruiting to improving airflow around your plants.

- *Selective Pruning:* Focus on removing any dead, diseased, or overcrowded branches and leaves. This not only improves the appearance of your plants but also enhances their health by increasing air circulation and light penetration.
- *Promote Fruiting and Flowering:* For certain plants, like tomatoes or peppers, pinching off some of the non-fruit-bearing branches can direct the plant's energy toward producing larger, healthier fruits.
- *Height Management:* For tall or vining plants, trimming them to maintain a manageable height can prevent them from overshadowing their shorter companions, ensuring all plants receive adequate sunlight.

Heat Stress Management

With the peak of summer heat, plants can experience stress, manifesting as wilting, leaf burn, or halted growth. Mitigating this stress calls for strategic action.

- *Shade Cloths:* Installing shade cloths over the most vulnerable plants during the hottest parts of the day can reduce temperature and light intensity, providing a much-needed respite.
- *Watering Schedule:* Adjusting your watering schedule to provide a deep soak less frequently encourages profound root growth, which helps plants access moisture from deeper within the soil during dry spells.
- *Plant Placement:* Consider the placement of your plants carefully. Those that are more tolerant of heat and sunlight can provide natural shade to more delicate companions, creating a microclimate that buffers against extreme conditions.

In summer, our gardens are at their most lively, but they also require vigilant care to navigate the challenges posed by intense heat and prolonged daylight. Adjusting our watering practices ensures our plants stay hydrated without succumbing to water waste or root issues. Mulching becomes an essential practice, acting as a cooling blanket that conserves moisture and protects against the baking sun. Pruning not only shapes our garden for beauty and balance but also promotes healthier, more productive plants. Lastly, managing heat stress through strategic shade, watering, and plant placement ensures our garden remains a thriving oasis even as the mercury rises. With these summer maintenance tips, your companion-planted garden will continue to flourish, offering a bounty of fruits, vegetables, and flowers through the season's warmth.

FALL PLANTING & PREPARATION

Autumn whispers through the garden, a reminder that the cycle of growth ebbs towards a quieter time. Yet, this season of mellow fruitfulness is ripe with opportunity for the companion gardener. It's a period to sow for the future, nurture the soil, and tidy the beds, ensuring a garden that wakes to spring vitality.

Fall Companion Planting Choices

The cooler days of fall don't signal an end but a transition. Some plants thrive in this chill, their growth invigorated by the crisp air:

- *Garlic and Strawberries:* As companions, garlic helps deter pests from strawberries, which can still bear fruit in mild autumns. Planting garlic in the fall lets it establish roots, ready for a spring flourish.
- *Spinach and Radishes:* Quick-growing radishes can mark spaces between spinach, which appreciates the cooling soil. Spinach, sown in late summer or early autumn, matures as a tender crop and often withstands winter's onset if given a little protection.

These pairings leverage the unique advantages of the season, providing fresh produce even as the year winds down.

Preparing for the First Frost

The first frost paints the garden with a crystalline touch, beautiful yet potentially harsh on tender plants. Some steps can help shield your companions from its bite:

- *Floating Row Covers:* Light, permeable fabrics placed over rows can fend off frost, trapping warmth. They're light enough to rest on the plants without causing damage, offering protection during chilly nights.
- *Water Before Frost:* Interestingly, watering your garden before a predicted frost can help protect plants. Moist soil holds warmth better than dry soil, offering a thermal buffer.

These simple actions can make an impactful difference, allowing your garden extra weeks of productivity.

Soil Enrichment

As plants give back with their bounty, autumn is a time to return the favor to the soil that sustains them. Enriching the garden now sets the stage for spring's awakening:

- *Compost Addition:* Spreading compost over garden beds in the fall allows it to integrate and enrich the soil over the winter months. This slow melding process ensures nutrients are readily available when plants next seek them.
- *Green Manures:* Fast-growing cover crops, such as clover or vetch, sown in emptied beds, act as green manures. They protect the soil from erosion and, when tilled in before spring, add organic matter and nutrients.

This care for the soil mirrors the cycle of giving and receiving inherent in nature, reinforcing the garden's vitality.

Clean-up and Pest Management

With the harvest gathered, cleaning the garden might seem like a closing ritual, yet it's a critical step for the garden's health:

- *Remove Spent Plants:* Clearing away dead or dying plants eliminates hiding spots for pests and diseases, reducing their chances in the next growing season.
- *Tidy the Beds:* Trimming perennials and removing invasive weeds prevents unwanted spread and competition for resources in the spring.
- *Pest Patrol:* Inspect your plants for signs of disease or infestation. Removing affected parts now can prevent the spread of issues. Consider natural deterrents or barriers for persistent problems, planning for their implementation next year.

This attentive tidying and vigilant pest management ensures the garden rests well, ready to rise again with the spring.

Autumn in the companion garden is a reflective time, a season to appreciate the year's growth and to prepare for the future. Choosing the right plants for late-season planting ensures the garden continues to offer its gifts, even as the days grow shorter. Preparing for the first frost, enriching the soil, and thoroughly cleaning up and managing pests are all acts of care that underscore the gardener's role not just as a cultivator of plants but also as a steward of the earth. Through these actions, the garden is poised for rest, its beds and borders a promise of the cycle to come.

WINTER CARE FOR RAISED BEDS & CONTAINERS

As the garden dons its winter cloak, a quiet descends, punctuated only by the crunch of frost underfoot. This season of rest is deceptive; beneath the surface, the garden is preparing for the resurgence of spring. For the gardener, winter becomes a time of protection and preparation, an opportunity to tend to the silent garden in anticipation of the year ahead.

Protecting Perennials

The resilience of perennials is one of the garden's greatest gifts, yet even these hardy plants benefit from a helping hand through the winter months. Here's how to ensure they emerge vibrant and healthy with the return of warmth:

- *Mulching Matters:* Applying a generous layer of mulch around your perennials acts like a snug blanket, insulating the soil and roots from sudden temperature changes that can be detrimental. Organic materials like straw or shredded leaves are ideal, offering not just warmth but also enriching the soil as it decomposes.
- *Wind Protection:* For those in particularly windy locales, creating windbreaks can prevent cold winds from drying and damaging plants. Strategically placed burlap screens can shield your garden without compromising airflow.
- *Pruning:* While heavy pruning is best left for spring, removing dead or diseased wood before winter can help prevent pests and diseases from popping up. This clean-up reduces the garden's vulnerability to winter's challenges.

Container Care in Winter

Containers add versatility to the garden but require special attention as temperatures drop. Their exposed surfaces leave roots more vulnerable to cold, demanding a strategy to guard against frost:

- *Insulation:* Wrapping containers in burlap or bubble wrap can provide critical insulation, helping to maintain a more stable root environment. For added protection, consider nestling containers together on a protected porch or against the house to buffer them from the elements.
- *Relocation:* Whenever possible, moving containers to a sheltered location, like a garage or shed, can offer respite from the harshest weather. Ensure these spaces are frost-free if plants are to remain there throughout the winter.
- *Drainage Check:* Before the onset of freezing weather, verify that containers have adequate drainage. Waterlogged pots can freeze, expanding the soil and potentially cracking containers.

Planning and Ordering Seeds

Winter's quiet is the perfect backdrop for dreaming up next year's garden. With catalogs in hand and websites bookmarked, consider how companion plants will share your space:

- *Reflect on the Past Year:* What combinations thrived? Were there pest challenges that different pairings could mitigate? This reflection guides your seed choices, leaning towards varieties that complement each other in growth habits, nutrient needs, and pest management.
- *Order Early:* Popular varieties sell out quickly. Placing orders now ensures you have your first choices ready for spring sowing. Pay special attention to companion plants that support each other, such as marigolds with tomatoes

for pest control or beans with corn for soil nitrogen enrichment.
- *Sketch Your Plan:* Drawing a rough layout of your garden beds or containers, noting where each plant or plant pair will go, can help visualize the garden's balance. This plan becomes a roadmap, guiding your activities once the planting season arrives.

Maintenance of Garden Tools

Tools are the gardener's trusted allies, deserving of care to keep them in good working order. Winter offers the time to tend to this often-overlooked task:

- *Cleaning:* Remove soil, rust, and plant debris from your tools. A stiff brush and soapy water can clean most items, while a sand and oil mixture can help remove rust.
- *Sharpening:* Sharp tools make garden work more efficient and less damaging to plants. Files and whetstones can sharpen blades, from pruners to shovels, ensuring they're ready for spring's workload.
- *Oil and Store:* Once clean and sharp, a small coat of oil on metal parts prevents rust. Store tools in a dry, protected place, such as a shed or garage, where they're organized and easily accessible come spring.

Winter, in its silence, holds the space for care and preparation. It's a time to protect what is and plan for what's to come, ensuring the garden and its caretakers are ready for the year ahead.

YEAR-ROUND HARVEST STRATEGIES

Creating a garden that produces food throughout the year requires a thoughtful approach, blending traditional knowledge with innovative techniques. It's about more than just planting and hoping for the best; it's a deliberate strategy to ensure your garden is as productive in the cooler months as it is at the height of summer.

Succession Planting

Succession planting is a method that ensures a steady supply of produce by staggering plantings throughout the growing season. Here's how to weave this strategy into your companion planting system:

- Start with a calendar and note the maturity times for each crop you plan to grow, alongside the last frost date in spring and the first frost date in fall.
- Plant seeds at intervals—every two weeks is a standard approach for many crops, such as lettuces, radishes, and carrots. This way, as one crop matures and is harvested, another is coming into its prime.
- Consider the companion plants that grow well together and how their harvest times can complement each other. For example, fast-growing radishes can be sown alongside slower-maturing carrots. By the time the carrots need more space, the radishes will have been harvested.

This strategy maximizes the use of space and maintains soil health, as different plants have varying nutrient needs and pest resistance. It keeps the soil balanced and productive.

Cold-Frame Gardening

Cold frames, essentially mini-greenhouses, can extend the growing season by protecting plants from the cold. They are handy for leafy greens and herbs that can survive with minimal warmth. Here's how to utilize them:

- Place your cold frame in a spot that gets ample winter sunlight and is shielded from harsh winds.
- Use it to shelter young plants started late in the season or to protect hardy greens and root vegetables, allowing them to continue growing into the colder months.
- Ventilate on sunny days to prevent overheating and condensation issues, which can cause mold and mildew.

Cold frames bridge the gap between fall and spring, offering a microclimate that nurtures growth even when the rest of the garden is dormant.

Crop Rotation

Rotating crops in a companion planting garden minimizes disease and balances soil nutrients. Each type of plant interacts with the soil differently, some consuming specific nutrients heavily, while others might add them back:

- Plan a rotation schedule that moves plant families to different areas of the garden each year. For instance, after growing tomatoes (a heavy feeder) in one spot, plant beans (a nitrogen fixer) there the next season to replenish the soil.
- Avoid planting the same family of crops (like nightshades: tomatoes, peppers, eggplants) in the same spot more than once every three or four years. This helps break cycles of pests and diseases that thrive on specific plants.

This strategy not only keeps the soil healthy but also encourages you to diversify your garden's plant life, enhancing its resilience and productivity.

Record-Keeping

Maintaining a garden journal is invaluable for refining your year-round harvest strategy. Record what you plant, where, and when, alongside observations on weather, pests, diseases, and harvest dates:

- Note successful plant pairings and those that didn't thrive, adjusting your plans for the next cycle accordingly.
- Track crop rotations to ensure you're not planting the same families in the same spots too frequently.
- Use your journal to plan succession plantings and staggering sowing dates based on previous years' experiences to ensure continuous harvests.

This written record becomes a treasure trove of insights, guiding your decisions and helping you adapt your strategies to the unique rhythms of your garden space.

By weaving these strategies together, from succession planting to utilizing cold frames, rotating crops, and keeping detailed records, you are crafting a garden that not only sustains itself but also provides a bounty across the seasons. This dynamic approach is responsive to the garden's changing needs and the gardener's growing knowledge. These practices lay the groundwork for a resilient garden ecosystem, one that adapts and thrives year-round, providing fresh produce even as the seasons turn.

As we close this exploration into year-round harvest strategies, it becomes clear that successful gardening is not just about the plants we choose or the techniques we employ. It's about understanding and working within the natural cycles of growth, decay, and renewal. It's a reminder that, in gardening, as in life, there's a time for everything—a time to plant, a time to harvest, and a time to rest and plan for the cycle to begin anew. With this chapter behind us, we look forward to delving deeper into the specificities of companion planting, ready to apply these overarching strategies to the intricate dance of interplant relationships in the chapters to come.

8

TROUBLESHOOTING: THE MOST COMMON GARDEN ISSUES

IMAGINE WALKING through your garden in the early morning, the dew still clinging to the leaves, the air filled with the promise of growth. You notice a tomato plant with leaves that look a little off or a squash plant that's not as robust as its companion. It's a moment every gardener faces – the realization that despite our best efforts, plants can encounter problems. But fear not! This chapter is all about equipping you with the know-how to identify and tackle common issues, ensuring your companion garden continues to thrive.

ADDRESSING COMMON PLANT DISEASES

Gardens are ecosystems teeming with life, and just like any living system, they can experience health issues. Here, we'll walk through identifying common plant diseases, preventive practices to keep your garden healthy, natural remedies for when problems arise, and the selection of disease-resistant plant varieties.

Disease Identification:

- *Powdery Mildew:* It appears on leaves as white powdery spots, often in humid conditions.
- *Blight:* Causes wilting, browning, and death of plant tissue.
- *Rust:* Recognizable by orange or brownish spots on leaves.
- *Each has distinct symptoms:* Yellowing leaves, stunted growth, or unusual spots can be general red flags.

Preventative Measures:

- *Crop Rotation:* Changing where you plant specific families of crops each year prevents the buildup of soil-borne diseases.
- *Proper Spacing:* Ensures good air circulation, reducing the risk of fungal infections.
- *Watering at Soil Level:* Keeps leaves dry and less susceptible to diseases.

Natural Remedies:

- *Baking Soda Spray:* Mixing baking soda and water is a gentle fungicide for issues like powdery mildew.
- *Milk Spray:* Surprisingly, spraying a mix of milk and water on susceptible plants can help prevent mildew diseases.
- *Neem Oil:* A natural pesticide that can help manage a variety of issues without harming beneficial insects.

Disease-Resistant Varieties:

- Many plant breeders have developed varieties that are resistant to common diseases. When planning your garden, look for these as a first line of defense. For example, several tomato varieties are bred for resistance to specific blights and wilts.

By understanding common plant diseases, implementing preventive measures, and using natural remedies, you can maintain a healthy companion garden. Opting for disease-resistant varieties further strengthens your garden's defenses, making it more resilient against potential threats. Equipped with this knowledge, you can enjoy the beauty and bounty of your garden with confidence, knowing you're prepared to address challenges as they arise.

Insect Identification Chart

Disease Control Guide For Vegetables

Scan Me!

SOLVING WATERING ISSUES

Water is the lifeblood of any garden, a truth that becomes especially poignant in companion planting, where the needs of one plant can vastly differ from those of its neighbor. Navigating these waters, so to speak, requires a nuanced approach, one that balances the requirements of each plant to create a harmonious living tapestry.

Signs of Over and Under-Watering

The symptoms of giving too much or too little water can sometimes mimic each other, leading to confusion. Here's how to tell them apart and what actions to take:

- *Over-Watering:* Leaves might turn a yellowish-green and feel soft to the touch, often wilting despite the wet soil. The key here is to allow the soil to dry out before watering again and to ensure your garden has proper drainage.
- *Under-Watering:* Leaves appear dry and brittle and may curl at the edges. The soil around the plant will feel dry to the touch. Gradual rehydration is the solution, starting with slow and deep watering to reach the roots where moisture is most needed.

Irrigation Strategies

While traditional watering methods have their place, companion gardening benefits from systems that can cater to the varied needs of closely planted companions.

- *Drip Systems:* These allow water to trickle slowly to the roots of each plant. It minimizes waste and ensures that each companion receives the moisture it needs without over-saturating others. Placing drip emitters according to the water requirement of each plant can make this system highly effective.
- *Self-Watering Containers:* Ideal for companion plants with similar water needs, these containers have a reservoir at the bottom that plants can draw moisture from as needed, reducing the risk of both over and under-watering.

Watering Best Practices

To ensure each plant receives just the right amount of water, consider the following:

- *Morning Watering:* Doing so helps reduce evaporation and gives the plants time to absorb water before the heat of the day.
- *Mulching:* Applying a layer of organic mulch will assist in retaining soil moisture and keep the roots cool. Don't forget to keep any mulch a few inches away from the stems to help avoid rot.
- *Watering at the Base:* This method reduces water waste and helps prevent leaf diseases by keeping foliage dry.

Troubleshooting Tips

Even with the best-laid plans, watering issues can arise. Here's how to tackle some common problems:

- *Uneven Water Distribution:* In gardens where companion plants have different water needs, consider using ollas or buried clay pots. Fill these with water, and they'll slowly release moisture into the soil, allowing plants to take what they need.
- *Hard, Compact Soil:* Sometimes water runs off rather than soaking in. Aerate your soil by gently loosening it without disturbing plant roots. Adding organic matter can also improve soil structure and water retention.
- *Waterlogged Soil:* For areas that don't drain well, consider raising your garden beds or incorporating more sand or perlite into your soil mix to improve drainage.

Water is a precious resource, and its reasonable use in the garden not only conserves this vital element but ensures your plants can grow in harmony, each with their unique needs met. Through careful observation, a bit of creativity, and the willingness to adjust practices as needed, the challenges of watering a companion garden become less daunting, transforming into another aspect of the joy of gardening.

NUTRIENT DEFICIENCIES AND HOW TO FIX THEM

In the dance of companion planting, where each plant plays off the strengths of its partners, maintaining a nutrient-rich environment becomes a delicate balancing act. At times, despite our best efforts, signs emerge that something is amiss beneath the soil's surface. Recognizing these signs early on and knowing how to address them can turn potential setbacks into opportunities for growth.

Recognizing Deficiencies

Each nutrient deficiency leaves its unique fingerprint on plant leaves, stems, or overall growth patterns. Being attuned to these signals is the first step in restoring balance:

- *Nitrogen (N):* Pale, yellow-green leaves, especially on older, lower leaves, and stunted growth are telltale signs. Nitrogen is crucial for leaf development and overall growth.
- *Phosphorus (P):* Dark, dull, or purple-tinged leaves and a lack of flower or fruit development indicate a phosphorus shortage, vital for energy transfer within the plant.
- *Potassium (K):* Symptoms include yellowing leaf edges, brown spotting, and weak stems. Potassium helps regulate water and resist disease.

- *Calcium (Ca):* New leaves may appear distorted or irregularly shaped, with blossom end rot in tomatoes being a common symptom. Calcium is critical for cell wall growth and structure.
- *Magnesium (Mg):* Older leaves show yellowing between veins, which may turn reddish-purple in severe cases. Magnesium is central to chlorophyll production.

Soil Testing and Amendments

A soil test is invaluable to pinpoint and address nutrient imbalances accurately. It can reveal not only which nutrients are lacking but also provide insights into soil pH, affecting nutrient availability. Here's how to proceed once you have your results:

- *Adjusting pH:* Lime can raise the pH of acidic soil, making it more alkaline, while sulfur can lower the pH of alkaline soil, making it more acidic. The correct pH range ensures nutrients are available to plants.
- *Amending Soil:* Based on test results, you can add specific amendments to balance deficiencies:
- *For Nitrogen:* Incorporate composted manure or a green manure crop like clover into the soil.
- *For Phosphorus:* Bone meal and rock phosphate can help boost phosphorus levels.
- *For Potassium:* Kelp meal or wood ash can be used to increase potassium.

Remember, amending soil is not a one-time task but part of ongoing garden care to maintain nutrient balance.

Companion Planting Solutions

Companion planting offers natural strategies to enhance nutrient uptake:

- *Nitrogen-Fixing Plants:* Legumes such as beans, peas, and more have a symbiotic relationship with rhizobia bacteria, converting atmospheric nitrogen into a form accessible to plants. Planting them alongside nitrogen-loving companions like corn can reduce the need for synthetic fertilizers.
- *Deep-Rooted Companions:* Plants like dandelions and chicory can mine the subsoil for nutrients, bringing them closer to the surface where shallower-rooted plants can benefit.
- *Dynamic Accumulators:* Certain plants, like comfrey and stinging nettle, are known for their ability to gather specific nutrients from the soil. When chopped and dropped as mulch or brewed into a nutrient-rich tea, they can share these benefits with their neighbors.

Organic Fertilization Options

When soil amendments and companion planting strategies need a boost, organic fertilizers can provide the necessary nutrients without harming the delicate relationships within your garden:

- *Compost:* The cornerstone of any organic garden, compost adds a wide array of nutrients and improves soil structure. Plus, it's something you can produce from your kitchen and garden waste.
- *Liquid Fish Emulsion:* Packed with nitrogen, phosphorus, and potassium, this fast-acting liquid fertilizer supports plant growth without risking chemical buildup in the soil.

- *Worm Castings:* Known as black gold in gardening circles, worm castings are a gentle yet powerful fertilizer that can enhance plant growth, soil structure, and microbial life.

By integrating these organic options into your garden care routine, you not only feed your plants but also nurture the soil life that supports them, creating a cycle of health and abundance that sustains your garden from one season to the next.

DEALING WITH OVERCROWDING

In the dance of companion planting, every plant has its role, its space to flourish and contribute to the garden's overall health and productivity. Yet, as in any lively gathering, things can get a bit crowded. Overcrowding not only hampers the growth of individual plants but can also lead to a cascade of challenges, from reduced air circulation to increased competition for light, water, and nutrients. Addressing this issue requires a blend of foresight, strategy, and, sometimes, a willingness to make tough decisions for the greater good of your garden.

Space Planning

The foundation of a well-organized garden is thoughtful space planning. This goes beyond simply knowing the mature size of a plant; it involves understanding how plants interact with each other, their growth habits, and their below-ground needs. Here's how you can keep overcrowding at bay right from the start:

- *Visualize Growth:* When planning your garden, visualize not just the sprouts but the full-grown plants. This helps in allocating enough space for each plant to expand without encroaching on its neighbors.

- *Understand Root Systems:* Some plants have deep taproots, while others spread out just below the surface. Knowing this can help you position plants in a way that their roots don't have to compete fiercely for nutrients and water.
- *Height and Spread:* Consider both the height and the spread of plants. Tall plants should be placed where they won't cast shade on shorter, sun-loving companions.

Pruning and Thinning Techniques

Sometimes, despite our best efforts, plants grow more vigorously than anticipated, or we get a little overzealous with seeding. Here's where pruning and thinning come into play:

- *Selective Thinning:* For densely sown crops like carrots or lettuce, thinning out the weakest seedlings early on gives the remaining plants room to develop fully. This might seem wasteful, but think of it as sacrificing a few for the benefit of many.
- *Pruning for Airflow and Light:* Regular pruning can prevent overcrowding, especially in bushy plants like tomatoes. Removing some inner branches improves air circulation and light penetration, which are crucial for reducing disease risk and encouraging even fruit ripening.

Replanting Strategies

At times, plants outgrow their designated spots or start to infringe on their companions' space. When this happens, replanting or transplanting can give all your plants the room they need:

- *Timing:* The best time to move a plant is during cooler parts of the day, preferably in the evening, so the plant has

time to settle in without the immediate stress of sun and heat.
- *Water Before and After:* Ensure the plant is well-watered before moving it, and water generously after replanting to help ease the transition and reduce transplant shock.
- *Root Protection:* When lifting a plant, aim to keep as much of the root ball intact as possible. This can help minimize stress on the plant and help it recover and regrow more quickly in its new location.

Preventative Measures

The best way to tackle overcrowding is to prevent it from happening in the first place. Here are some strategies to ensure your garden remains spacious and airy:

- *Adhere to Spacing Guidelines:* Resist the temptation to squeeze in just one more plant. Stick to the spacing recommendations for each species, considering their mature size.
- *Choose Varieties Wisely:* Opt for plant varieties that are well-suited to your space. Dwarf or compact varieties can be just as productive as their larger counterparts but take up less room.
- *Plan for Succession Planting:* Instead of planting all your seeds at once, stagger plantings throughout the season. This approach not only prevents overcrowding but also extends your harvest period.

By giving each plant the space it needs to grow, you're not just preventing overcrowding; you're promoting a healthier, more productive garden. Thoughtful space planning, regular maintenance through pruning and thinning, the strategic relocating of plants, and preemptive measures to manage plant growth ensure that every part of your garden gets the light, air, and nutrients it needs to thrive. With these practices in place, your garden becomes a dynamic yet harmoniously balanced ecosystem where every plant supports and is supported by its companions.

REBALANCING YOUR GARDEN'S ECOSYSTEM

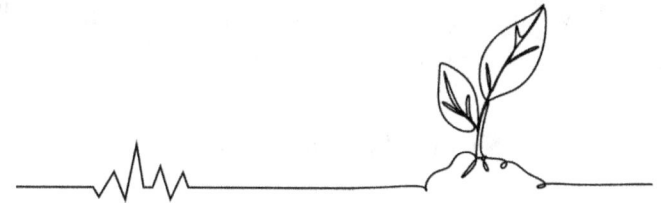

Gardens are living tapestries where each thread, plant, and creature plays a role in the overall health and beauty of the scene. When this balance tips, it's noticeable: plants might not thrive as they should, pests could become frequent visitors, and the garden, in general, might seem a little off-kilter. Recognizing the signs of such imbalances is the first step towards restoring harmony. Look out for increased disease susceptibility, a noticeable decrease in pollinators, or a single species of insect becoming too dominant. These are indicators that the ecosystem might need a little help getting back on track.

Identifying Imbalances

Observation is your greatest tool in the garden. A sudden outbreak of aphids on your roses, for example, might not just be a standalone issue but a symptom of broader ecological shifts. Similarly, if your soil starts to seem more compacted or your compost isn't breaking down as efficiently, these, too, can be signs that the balance is off.

Biodiversity as a Solution

Introducing a wider variety of plants is akin to opening new channels of communication within your garden's ecosystem. Each plant attracts and supports different beneficial insects and contributes differently to soil health. Adding native plants can be particularly effective, as these are already adapted to local conditions and support local wildlife. Consider diversifying not just the types of plants but also their flowering times to provide resources for pollinators throughout the growing season.

Natural Pest Management

Chemical interventions often act like a sledgehammer, disrupting more than just the pests they target. By contrast, natural pest control methods are more like surgical strikes, addressing problems without upsetting the garden's balance. Introducing natural predators, such as ladybugs for aphids, can help manage pest populations. Another effective strategy is interplanting with aromatic herbs, many of which repel unwanted insects while attracting beneficial ones.

Plant health is inherently tied to the health of its ecosystem. Healthy, vigorous plants are less likely to succumb to pests and diseases. Practices such as mulching, proper watering, and regular weeding go a long way in maintaining this vigor. Beyond these, fostering a habitat for wildlife, from birds to beneficial insects, creates a self-regulating garden, reducing the need for human intervention.

Long-Term Ecosystem Health

Sustaining a garden's ecosystem requires a commitment to observation and a willingness to adapt. Soil health, for instance, is fundamental. Regularly adding organic matter through compost or mulch not only feeds the soil but also encourages a lively community of microorganisms essential for a healthy garden ecosystem. Crop rotation and allowing areas of the garden to rest or grow green manures are practices that contribute to soil vitality and prevent the depletion of nutrients.

Water conservation strategies, like rainwater harvesting and drip irrigation, will ensure that the garden thrives even in less-than-ideal conditions. These practices, combined with a thoughtful approach to garden planning, where the needs and benefits of each plant are considered, create a resilient garden ecosystem.

Finally, embracing a philosophy of minimal intervention allows the garden to find its own equilibrium. This doesn't mean neglect but rather a conscious decision to let nature lead the way, stepping in only when necessary. It's about trusting in the natural resilience and adaptive capacity of the living garden, supporting its health through sustainable practices, and enjoying the bounty and beauty it offers in return.

Remember that the true essence of gardening lies in connection with the living world around us. It's about creating spaces where life in all its forms can thrive, finding joy in the dance of insects among the flowers, the rustle of leaves in the wind, and the rich scent of healthy soil. This connection, this celebration of life, is what makes a garden truly vibrant. As we move forward, we carry with us the knowledge that our actions, big and small, shape the world beneath our feet and the air around us, crafting a legacy of harmony and abundance for generations to come.

9

NURTURING THE FOUNDATION: SOIL & SUSTAINABILITY

IN A WORLD where every spoonful of soil holds the potential for growth, establishing a harmonious relationship with this fundamental resource is more than gardening—it's a dialogue with nature. Think of composting not as recycling plant leftovers but as stirring a cauldron of life, transforming the ordinary into the extraordinary.

It's about seeing fallen leaves not as debris but as future soil, ripe with the promise of nurturing the next generation of plants. This chapter dives into the earthy essence of composting, an alchemy that turns the end of one life cycle into the beginning of another, enriching our gardens and, by extension, our lives.

Basics of Composting

Composting is nature's way of recycling, a process where organic material breaks down into a rich substance that feeds the soil and, in turn, our plants. It's a balance of green materials like kitchen scraps and garden trimmings, which provide nitrogen, and brown materials, such as dead leaves and shredded paper, offering carbon. The magic ratio? Aim for about two-thirds brown to one-third green. This mix invites a host of microorganisms to do their work, breaking down the materials into compost that's black gold for gardens.

On the next page you will find a composting chart to get you started!

Compost Systems for Small Spaces

No sprawling backyard? No problem. Composting doesn't demand vast spaces. A tumbler, a compact, sealed container that you turn manually, fits snugly in a corner, speeding up the composting process with its efficient mixing and aeration. Then there's vermicomposting, where red wiggler worms transform scraps into compost, all within a container that can live under a sink. These systems are perfect for small gardens and patios, proving that even the smallest spaces can contribute to the cycle of growth. If you don't want to buy a tumbler or have a worm farm, you can set up your own compost pile in your backyard or make a DIY compost container.

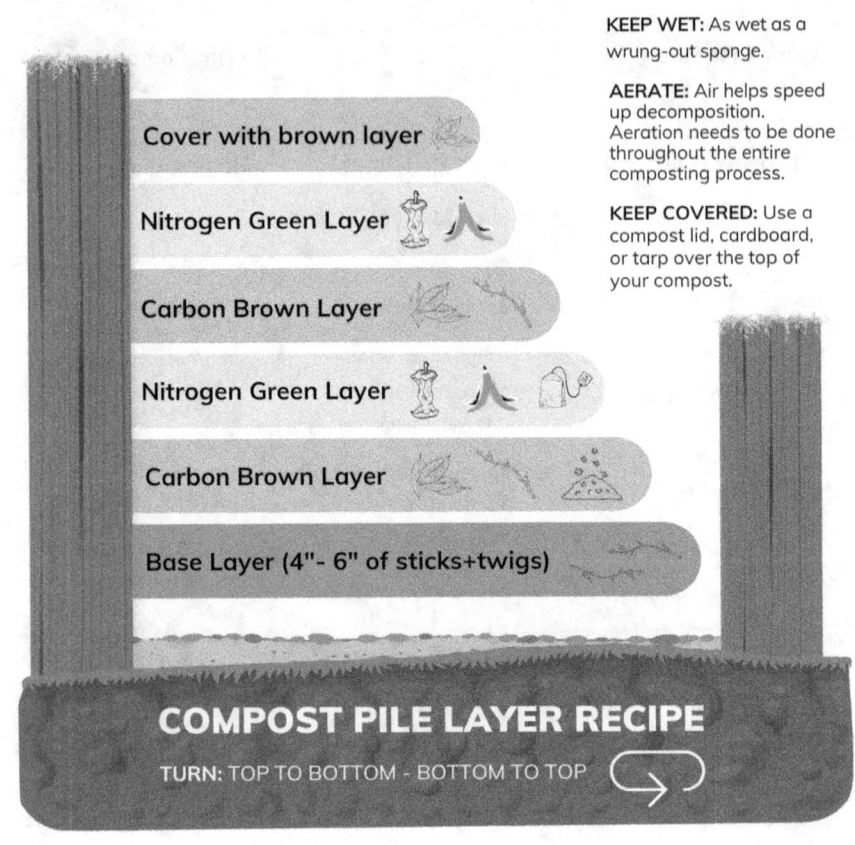

Benefits to Companion Plants

For companion plants, compost is a lifeline. It slowly releases nutrients, accessible when plants need them, unlike synthetic fertilizers that can overwhelm and burn plants. Compost also improves soil structure, making it easier for roots to grow, and enhances soil's water retention, which is crucial for companions that share a bed. Think of adding compost to your garden as laying down a feast for your plants, where every nutrient sparks growth, resilience, and productivity.

Troubleshooting Common Composting Problems

Even the best-laid compost piles can encounter hiccups. A compost pile that smells more like a landfill than earthy soil likely has too much green material, tipping the nitrogen balance. The fix? Add more browns like dry leaves or straws. If your compost is too dry and slow to decompose, it's craving more greens or a bit of moisture. And those uninvited pests? Ensure your compost bin is sealed correctly, and avoid adding oils, meats, or dairy products that attract rodents and flies.

On the next page you will find a chart to help you identify and remedy the most common composting problems!

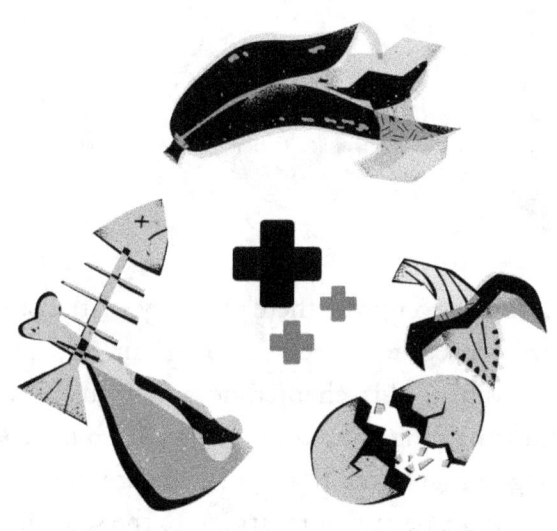

Issue	Qucik Remedy	Long-Term Solution
The material does not decompose (It is dense & there is no change after 2 weeks)	Use a rake or pitchfork to poke air holes.	Give it constant aeration.
Compost is too wet (Lots of moisture and bad odor)	Add dry browns.	Change location, air it out often, and add browns until consistent.
Browns are not breaking down (no heat, moisture & no sign of active life forms)	Add greens & water until the pile is moist.	Keep a good balance of browns to greens (can vary).
Compost is too hot (looks smoky or burnt)	Add water and mix until moist.	Maintain a balanced browns-to-greens ratio. Avoid excess greens & aerate often.
No active organisms (no insects or microorganisms)	Add soil from a thriving compost pile. Rethink your greens & browns.	Add 250-300 red wiggler warms, or fresh horse/cow manure.

In every handful of compost, there's a story of transformation, of cycles that turn waste into wonder, feeding our gardens in the most natural way possible. This chapter not only guides you through creating and maintaining your compost system but also illuminates compost's integral role in the health of companion-planted gardens. It's a testament to the beauty of returning to the soil what came from it, closing the loop in a sustainable, nourishing dance of life.

CREATING A SEED SAVING PLAN

Saving seeds, a tradition as old as agriculture itself connects us to the cycles of growth and renewal. This practice, when woven into the fabric of companion planting, not only enhances the biodiversity of our gardens but also deepens our engagement with the dynamic ecosystem at our doorstep. Let's explore the steps to preserve the vitality of our gardens through seed saving.

Selecting Plants for Seed Saving

Choosing suitable candidates for seed saving is crucial. Heirloom and open-pollinated varieties are the stars in this arena, revered for their ability to produce offspring true to type. These plants have weathered the test of time, adapting to local conditions and thriving without the need for constant human intervention. When selecting plants for seed saving:

- Look for robust health, vigor, and outstanding qualities in flavor or resistance to pests and diseases. These traits, once captured in seeds, promise a lineage of hardy plants for seasons to come.
- Pay attention to pollination methods. Plants like tomatoes and beans self-pollinate, making them straightforward choices for seed saving. Others, such as squash, rely on insects for pollination and may require strategies to prevent unwanted cross-pollination.

Techniques for Harvesting and Storing Seeds

Harvesting and storing seeds with care ensures their viability for future planting. Each plant demands a unique approach, but the principles of patience and gentle handling unite them all.

- *Dry Seed Harvesting:* For plants like lettuce and carrots, wait until the seed heads are brown and dry. Gently remove the seeds and let them air dry on a clean surface for a week.

Remember to keep them away from direct sunlight for a week.
- *Wet Seed Processing:* Fleshy fruits such as tomatoes require a bit more work. Scoop out the seeds and pulp into a jar of water and let it ferment for a few days. This process separates the viable seeds, which sink, from the pulp and non-viable seeds, which float. Rinse the good seeds and spread them to dry.

Storing seeds in a dark, cool, and dry place preserves their germination capacity. Envelopes, glass jars, or metal tins work well, but ensure they're labeled with the plant name and date of harvest. Silica gel packets can be added to prevent moisture, extending seed life.

Benefits of Seed Saving

The rewards of seed saving extend far beyond the joy of watching a plant emerge from a seed you've saved.

- *Cost Savings:* By saving seeds, you reduce the need to purchase new ones each season, allowing you to allocate resources elsewhere in your garden.
- *Preserving Genetic Diversity:* Each seed saved is a living library of genetic material, contributing to the biodiversity that is crucial for resilient ecosystems.
- *Adaptation:* Seeds saved from plants that have thrived in your garden are likely to produce offspring well-suited to your specific microclimate and soil conditions, enhancing garden health and productivity over time.

Incorporating Seed Saving into Companion Planting

Integrating seed saving with companion planting magnifies the benefits of both practices.

- When planning your garden, consider spatial arrangements and timing to minimize unwanted cross-pollination. Physical barriers, such as planting tall crops between varieties prone to cross-pollinate, can be effective.
- Employ temporal separation by staggering planting times to ensure that only one variety of flowers and sets, seed at any given time, reducing the risk of cross-pollination.
- Label plants from which you intend to save seeds clearly, and consider dedicating a section of your garden to seed production. This will allow you to give these plants the special attention they need.

Incorporating seed saving into companion planting not only enriches the garden's biodiversity but also fosters a deeper connection between the gardener and the garden. Through careful selection, harvesting, and storage, gardeners can ensure a continuous cycle of growth that honors the past while nurturing the future. This symbiotic relationship between plants and gardeners, rooted in the practice of seed saving, promises a garden that is not only productive but also a vibrant testament to the cycles of nature.

ENCOURAGING NATURAL PREDATORS

In the tapestry of a garden, every creature plays its role, weaving a web of balance and productivity. It's in this intricate dance that we find the natural predators, the unsung heroes keeping pest populations in check. Their presence is a testament to a healthy ecosystem, a sign that our gardens are vibrant habitats supporting life in all its forms.

Identifying Beneficial Predators

Our gardens are bustling with activity, much of it beneath our notice. Yet, among the foliage and flowers, beneficial predators go about their crucial work. These include:

- *Ladybugs:* Voracious consumers of aphids, mites, and scale insects, ladybugs are a gardener's best friend. Just one ladybug can devour up to 50 aphids a day, making them invaluable in managing these common pests.
- *Lacewings:* Lacewings are another ally in the fight against pests. They are hungry for aphids, mite eggs, and caterpillars. Their larvae, in particular, are efficient hunters, working diligently to keep populations low.
- *Predatory Mites:* These tiny creatures are formidable opponents of spider mites, a common nuisance in gardens. By introducing predatory mites, you can protect your plants from mite infestations without resorting to chemical treatments.

Each of these predators brings a unique set of skills to the garden. They target specific pests and contribute to the overall health of the ecosystem.

Attracting Predators to Your Garden

Creating a garden that welcomes these beneficial creatures is simpler than you might think. The key lies in diversity and providing the right habitats. Consider these strategies:

- *Plant Diversity:* A variety of plants attracts a broader range of insects, including beneficial predators. Incorporate flowering plants like marigolds and sunflowers, which offer

nectar and pollen to adult insects, encouraging them to stay and hunt in your garden.
- *Insect Hotels:* These structures offer shelter for a variety of beneficial insects. Made from bundles of bamboo, straw, or even hollowed-out logs, insect hotels can be a cozy refuge for predators like lacewings and ladybugs.
- *Water Sources:* A simple birdbath or a shallow dish filled with stones and water provides a drinking spot for beneficial insects, encouraging them to make your garden their home.

By cultivating an environment that meets the needs of these predators, you're not just inviting them into your garden; you're offering them a place to thrive.

Maintaining a Predator-Friendly Environment

Once you've invited these natural allies into your garden, the next step is ensuring they want to stay. This means creating a space that supports their lifecycle and health.

- *Avoid Pesticides:* Even organic or natural pesticides can harm beneficial insects. Instead, focus on physical pest control methods, like hand-picking or using barriers, to manage outbreaks without disrupting your garden's natural defenders.
- *Provide Food Sources:* Beyond pest prey, many beneficial insects need nectar and pollen at different life stages. Incorporating flowering herbs like dill, fennel, and cilantro can offer sustenance to these crucial allies.
- *Leave Some Pests:* This might seem counterintuitive, but maintaining a small population of pests provides a

consistent food source for predators, preventing them from moving on in search of sustenance.

Creating a garden that supports beneficial predators is about more than just pest control; it's about fostering a living, breathing ecosystem right in your backyard.

Balancing Predator and Prey

The dance between predator and prey is delicate, a balance that shifts with the seasons and the health of the garden. Embracing this natural cycle means accepting that some pests will always be part of the garden landscape. The goal is not eradication but management, keeping pest populations at levels where they do minimal damage while serving as food for beneficial predators.

- *Monitor and Adjust:* Keep an eye on both pest and predator populations, stepping in to manage pests only when they threaten to overwhelm your plants. This might involve temporary barriers or selective removal of heavily infested plants.
- *Encourage Biodiversity:* The more diverse your garden, the more stable the ecosystem. This diversity helps prevent any one pest population from exploding, as there are more natural checks in place to keep them in balance.

By respecting and nurturing the natural balance between predators and prey, you allow your garden to become a self-regulating oasis, teeming with life and productivity. This approach not only reduces the need for intervention but also enriches the garden, making it a sanctuary for all manner of life.

WATER CONSERVATION TIPS

In the heart of a thriving garden, water dances from the sky and seeps from the earth, a precious resource that sustains life. In companion planting, understanding and optimizing water use goes beyond mere irrigation—it's about crafting a symbiotic relationship between plants to share this vital resource  efficiently. This part of our exploration into the nurturing world of gardens focuses on strategies that not only save water but also enhance the health and productivity of our plant companions.

Water-Saving Companion Pairings

When plants share space, they can also benefit from each other's presence, including efficient water use. Some plants naturally require less water and, when paired with those with similar needs, create an environment that conservatively uses water without sacrificing the garden's vibrancy.

- *Succulents and Mediterranean Herbs:* Pairing succulents with herbs like rosemary, thyme, and lavender, which thrive in dry conditions, ensures that none of the precious water goes to waste.
- *Shade Providers and Moisture Lovers:* Planting tall, leafy greens like kale or Swiss chard alongside moisture-loving plants such as lettuce helps reduce evaporation by providing natural shade, allowing the soil to retain moisture longer.

This approach not only conserves water but also encourages you to think creatively about plant relationships, turning your garden into a model of efficiency and harmony.

Mulching Techniques for Water Retention

Mulch acts as a protective blanket for the soil, reducing evaporation, moderating soil temperature, and adding an aesthetic touch to the garden beds. The choice of mulch and its application play a crucial role in water conservation within a companion planting setup.

- *Organic Mulches:* Straw, shredded bark, and leaf mold are excellent choices, enriching the soil as they decompose. Apply a layer of about 2-4 inches around plants, taking care not to pile it against stems to avoid rot.
- *Inorganic Mulches:* Gravel or pebbles can be used around plants that prefer warmer soil temperatures. Though they don't enrich the soil, they excel at retaining moisture and deterring weeds.

The right mulch not only keeps the garden looking tidy but acts as a critical ally in conserving water, making every drop count.

Irrigation Efficiency

Efficient irrigation systems are the cornerstone of water conservation in the garden. Drip irrigation stands out for its ability to provide water directly to the root zone of plants, minimizing waste and ensuring that water goes precisely where it's needed.

- *Drip Irrigation Layout:* Installing a drip system in a companion planting garden can be customized to accommodate the varying water needs of different plants.

Emitters can be placed strategically to deliver more water to thirstier companions and less to those with lower requirements.
- *Timing and Automation:* Using timers can automate the irrigation process, ensuring plants are watered during the cooler times of the day to reduce evaporation. Even simple timers can make a significant difference in water usage efficiency.

Adopting these systems might require an initial investment of time and resources, but the payoff in water savings and healthier plants is invaluable.

Rainwater Harvesting

Capturing rainwater is an ancient practice that modern gardeners are rediscovering for its simplicity and sustainability. Rainwater harvesting systems can range from basic rain barrels connected to downspouts to more elaborate cisterns and storage tanks. Utilizing this naturally soft and chemical-free water source benefits plants and reduces dependence on treated municipal supplies.

- *Setting Up a Rain Barrel:* Placing a rain barrel under a downspout is an easy way to start harvesting rainwater. Ensure the barrel is covered to prevent debris and mosquitoes from getting in and use a fine mesh screen to filter the water as it enters.
- *Landscape Design for Water Capture:* Designing your garden landscape to direct runoff into planting areas or rain gardens allows you to make the most of natural rainfall, reducing the need for supplemental watering.

Integrating rainwater harvesting into your garden plan not only conserves water but also ties your gardening practices back to the natural cycles of the environment, creating a garden that's both productive and sustainable.

In weaving these water conservation strategies into the fabric of companion planting, we cultivate gardens that are not only lush and productive but also resilient and in harmony with the broader ecosystem. Through thoughtful pairings, efficient mulching, and innovative irrigation practices, we ensure that every drop of water serves a purpose, nurturing our plants and the soil they grow in. And by harnessing the bounty of the rain, we close the loop, creating gardens that thrive on the gifts of nature, sustaining not just themselves but the world around them.

LONG-TERM GARDEN PLANNING

Embarking on a gardening adventure is akin to nurturing a living, breathing entity, where each decision impacts not only the present but also the future. In this light, our focus turns toward strategies that ensure our gardens not only thrive today but continue to flourish for years to come.

Planning for Perennial Companions

Integrating perennial plants into companion planting arrangements adds layers of depth and resilience to our gardens. These steadfast companions offer a backbone of stability amidst the seasonal ebb and flow of annuals. When plotting their place in the garden:

- Consider the mature size and growth habits to ensure harmonious coexistence with neighboring plants. Perennials like asparagus and rhubarb need room to spread without overshadowing smaller companions.

- Reflect on the symbiotic relationships between perennials and annuals. For example, planting garlic near roses can help deter pests that prey on the flowers.
- Remember, some perennials, such as many herbs, also offer the bonus of attracting beneficial insects while deterring pests, doubling their value in the garden landscape.

Soil Health Maintenance

The vitality of our garden ecosystem hinges profoundly on the health of the soil. A few practices stand out for their ability to nurture this foundation:

- *Crop Rotation:* Regularly changing the types of plants grown in specific areas of the garden prevents nutrient depletion and disrupts pest and disease cycles. This simple practice keeps the soil balanced and plants healthy.
- *Cover Cropping:* Planting cover crops like clover and vetch in off-seasons protects and enriches the soil. These living mulches fix nitrogen, add organic matter, and prevent erosion, bolstering soil fertility for future plantings.
- *Adding Organic Matter:* Regular amendments with compost, leaf mold, or manure keep the soil rich in essential nutrients and microorganisms. This ongoing nourishment supports a vibrant, productive garden.

Observation and Adaptation

A gardener's most valuable tool is their powers of observation. Watching the garden's rhythms and responses reveals much about its needs and challenges.

- Note how plants respond to changes in weather, watering, and companion pairings. This insight guides adjustments to maximize health and yield.
- Stay flexible and ready to pivot strategies based on what the garden tells you. Sometimes, a plant thought to be a perfect companion might not thrive as expected, prompting a change in plans.
- Keep a garden journal to track observations, successes, and lessons learned. This record becomes a priceless reference that informs future gardening seasons.

Community Sharing and Learning

Gardening, at its heart, is a communal activity enriched by the exchange of knowledge and resources.

- Share seeds, cuttings, and harvests with neighbors and fellow garden enthusiasts. This generosity fosters a sense of community and encourages biodiversity.
- Participate in local gardening groups or online forums. The collective wisdom found in these communities can offer new perspectives and solutions to common challenges.
- Consider collaborative gardening projects that benefit the wider community, such as community gardens or educational workshops. These initiatives spread the joy and benefits of gardening, creating ripples of positive impact.

In weaving these threads together — from the thoughtful inclusion of perennials to the diligent care for soil health, the keen eye for observation, and the heart for community engagement — we cultivate gardens that are not just spaces of individual endeavor but vibrant ecosystems connected to a larger narrative of sustainability and resilience. As we tend to our gardens with an eye toward the future, we plant the seeds for a legacy of abundance, diversity, and shared joy that transcends the seasons.

As this exploration of long-term planning and sustainability draws to its conclusion, it's clear that the principles guiding our gardening efforts are deeply intertwined with the broader tapestry of life. The lessons learned in the garden — patience, observation, adaptability, and the importance of community — echo far beyond the boundaries of our plots, offering insights into living harmoniously with the natural world. With these foundations in place, we look forward to the next chapter in our gardening journey, ready to take on new challenges and opportunities with open hearts and minds.

BONUS

OUTRO

Well, you've done it! You've journeyed from the germinating seed of curiosity about companion planting to cultivating a flourishing garden that's as nourishing for the soul as it is for the body and the planet. Together, we've dug into the rich soil of gardening wisdom, planting pairs that sing in harmony, and setting up those first raised beds or container gardens that are now home to a vibrant tapestry of life.

From the roots of understanding the basics to the blossoms of mastering advanced techniques like ensuring a year-round harvest and creating an ecosystem where plants fend off pests and nurture each other, you've grown. And just like the best gardens, this journey has been about more than just the plants. It's been about fostering a healthier lifestyle, contributing to a sustainable environment, and deepening your connection to the incredible world under our feet and all around us.

But don't hang up your gardening gloves just yet. Gardening is a lifelong learning adventure, and I hope you're as excited as I am to see what's around the next bend. The path of a gardener is a winding one, full of new discoveries and challenges to overcome. There's always another companion pair to try, another natural mystery to unravel.

Now, it's time to take the next step. Whether it's expanding your garden, trying a new plant pairing, or teaching someone else about the magic of companion planting, there's so much more to do. And I want to thank you, truly, for letting me be a part of your gardening journey. Your commitment to turning a patch of earth into a thriving, life-affirming space is inspiring.

I'd love to hear about your adventures in gardening – the triumphs, the challenges, and everything in between. Share your stories, photos, and tips on social media or gardening forums. You never know who you might inspire to start their own journey into companion planting and organic gardening.

As we close this chapter (literally and figuratively), remember that every seed planted, every companion pair nurtured, is a step towards a greener, more vibrant world. You're not just growing plants; you're cultivating joy, health, and sustainability. So keep planting, keep experimenting, and keep growing, not just in your garden but in life.

Here's to the gardens we still need to grow and the discoveries we still need to make. Happy gardening!

REFERENCES

Fischer, N. (n.d.). Ancient Companion Planting: The Three Sisters. Nannie Appleseed. Retrieved from https://medium.com/nannie-appleseed/ancient-companion-planting-the-three-sisters-e1d3b5f34285

University of California Agriculture & Natural Resources. (n.d.). Better Together: The New Science of "Companion Planting". Retrieved from https://ucanr.edu/blogs/blogcore/postdetail.cfm?postnum=53468

University of Minnesota Extension. (n.d.). Companion Planting in home gardens. Retrieved from https://extension.umn.edu/planting-and-growing-guides/companion-planting-home-gardens

West Virginia University Extension. (n.d.). Companion Planting. Retrieved from https://extension.wvu.edu/lawn-gardening-pests/gardening/garden-management/companion-planting

National Garden Bureau. (n.d.). 7 Benefits of Raised Bed Gardening. Retrieved from https://ngb.org/raised-bed-gardening-benefits/

Savvy Gardening. (n.d.). DIY Potting Soil: 6 Homemade Potting Mix Recipes for the ... Retrieved from https://savvygardening.com/diy-potting-soil/

Mostardi Nursery. (n.d.). *Vertical Gardening for Small Spaces*. Retrieved from https://mostardi.com/vertical-gardening-for-small-spaces/

The Free Range Life. (n.d.). *16 Ways to Use Companion Planting for Pest Control*. Retrieved from https://thefreerangelife.com/companion-planting-to-control-pests-naturally/

Gardenia.net. (n.d.). *Nitrogen-Fixing Plants to Enrich your Soil*. Retrieved from https://www.gardenia.net/guide/nitrogen-fixing-plants-to-enrich-soil

Royal Horticultural Society. (n.d.). *Study finds top 5 ways to provide for pollinators in urban*. Retrieved from https://www.rhs.org.uk/science/articles/urban-nectar-provision

Planet Natural. (n.d.). *Allelopathic Plants & Types of Allelopathy*. Retrieved from https://www.planetnatural.com/allelopathy/

Durham County Master Gardeners. (2018, April 25). *Best Practices for Container Gardening*. Retrieved from https://durhammastergardeners.com/2018/04/25/best-practices-for-container-gardening/

Mother Earth News. (n.d.). *An In-Depth Companion Planting Guide*. Retrieved twice, note for unique citation format.

Rodale Institute. (n.d.). *Choosing the Best Cover Crops for Your Organic No-Till ...* Retrieved from https://rodaleinstitute.org/science/articles/choosing-the-best-cover-crops-for-your-organic-no-till-vegetable-system/

Gardening.org. (n.d.). *20 Best Companion Plants to Grow for Natural Pest Control*. Retrieved from https://gardening.org/best-companion-plants-to-grow-for-natural-pest-control/

Mother Earth Gardener. (n.d.). *Companion Planting to Maximize Garden Space*. Retrieved from https://www.motherearthgardener.com/

organic-gardening/companion-planting-to-maximize-garden-space-zb0z1805/

The Spruce. (n.d.). 20 Edible Flowers You Can Grow in Your Garden. Retrieved from https://www.thespruce.com/edible-flowers-1403398

University of Wisconsin-Extension. (n.d.). Plant Flowers to Encourage Beneficial Insects. Retrieved from https://hort.extension.wisc.edu/articles/plant-flowers-to-encourage-beneficial-insects/

PictureThis AI. (n.d.). Boosting Your Yield: The Power of Vertical Companion Planting. Retrieved from https://www.picturethisai.com/blog/vertical-edible-gardening/Boosting-Your-Yield-The-Power-of-Vertical-Companion-Planting.html

The Tenth Acre Farm. (n.d.). How to Build a Permaculture Fruit Tree Guild. Retrieved from https://www.tenthacrefarm.com/how-to-build-a-fruit-tree-guild/

Colorado State University Extension. (n.d.). Drip Irrigation for Home Gardens - 4.702. Retrieved from https://extension.colostate.edu/topic-areas/yard-garden/drip-irrigation-home-gardens-4-702/

University of Hawaii at Manoa, College of Tropical Agriculture and Human Resources. (n.d.). Mulches for Pest Control and Soil Health. Retrieved from https://www.ctahr.hawaii.edu/uhmg/news/V17-Maris

Homes & Gardens. (n.d.). How to make plant fertilizer: 7 natural methods to try. Retrieved from https://www.homesandgardens.com/gardens/how-to-make-plant-fertilizer

Journey With Jill. (2019, February 26). Companion Planting for Pest Control. Retrieved from https://journeywithjill.net/gardening/2019/02/26/companion-planting-pest-control/

The Micro Gardener. (n.d.). 17 Water Saving Tips for Container Gardens. Retrieved from https://themicrogardener.com/17-water-saving-tips-container-gardens/

Roots and Refuge. (n.d.). *Organic Garden Pest Control*. Retrieved from https://rootsandrefuge.com/organic-garden-pest-control/

University of Minnesota Extension. (n.d.). *Extending the growing season in your garden*. Retrieved from https://extension.umn.edu/yard-and-garden-news/extending-growing-season-your-garden

Royal Horticultural Society. (n.d.). *Nutrient deficiencies*. Retrieved from https://www.rhs.org.uk/prevention-protection/nutrient-deficiencies

Growing in the Garden. (n.d.). *Best Way to Water Raised-Bed Gardens*. Retrieved from https://growinginthegarden.com/best-way-to-water-raised-bed-gardens/

Royal Botanic Gardens, Kew. (n.d.). *Top tips for a biodiverse garden*. Retrieved from https://www.kew.org/read-and-watch/how-to-make-your-garden-more-biodiverse

U.S. Environmental Protection Agency. (n.d.). *Composting At Home*. Retrieved from https://www.epa.gov/recycle/composting-home

University of California Agriculture & Natural Resources. (n.d.). *How to Get an Army of Beneficial Insects to Protect Your Garden*. Retrieved from https://ucanr.edu/blogs/blogcore/postdetail.cfm?postnum=48972

Perennial Companion Plants. (n.d.). *PerennialCo*. Retrieved from https://www.perennialco.com/blog/companion-plants/

www.ingramcontent.com/pod-product-compliance
Lightning Source LLC
Chambersburg PA
CBHW070426010526
44118CB00014B/1919